FADING AWAY: THE EXPERIENCE OF TRANSITION IN FAMILIES WITH TERMINAL ILLNESS

Betty Davies, RN, PhD
University of British Columbia
and
British Columbia's Children's Hospital

Joanne Chekryn Reimer, RN, MN
Canuck Place—A Hospice for Children
Vancouver, British Columbia

Pamela Brown, RN, MSN
Calgary, Alberta

Nola Martens, RN, MN
Families in Supportive Care Project
Sherwood Park, Alberta

Death, Value and Meaning Series
Series Editor, John D. Morgan

Baywood Publishing Company, Inc.
AMITYVILLE, NEW YORK

Library of Congress Catalog Number: 95-7705
ISBN: 0-89503-127-2 (paper)

Library of Congress Cataloging-in-Publication Data

Fading away : the experience of transition in families with terminal
   illness / Betty Davies . . . [et al.].
      p.   cm. - - (Death, value, and meaning series)
   Includes bibliographical references.
   ISBN 0-89503-127-2 (pbk.)
   1. Cancer- -Patients- -Family relationships.   2. Terminal care.
3. Terminally ill- -Family relationships.   I. Davies, Betty.
II. Series.
RC262.F33   1995
362.1'96994'0019- -dc20   95-7705
                                                              CIP

Preface

You think cancer and you think death . . . you can't erase that. And, if I didn't have a family, if it was just me, I don't think I'd even bother.

Mr J., age sixty-three, with lung cancer

What would help this man in his personal journey with serious illness and death? How do his intimate interconnections and interdependence with his family influence his care? How do practitioners support both him and his family as they face the imminent death of both the patient and the family as they have known it? These are the questions that plagued the staff of a regional cancer center and two of the researchers as they initiated a new supportive care program. They recognized that care of persons with cancer does not stop with treatment or cure. They appreciated that care must be family focused. However, they realized that their skills in meeting the needs of the families were limited.

At the same time, an impetus was growing for establishing a nursing research program within the center. A meeting was called to discuss ways to initiate such a program, and to identify potential research questions. The nurses' major concern was how to provide family focused palliative care. They were constantly having to attend to the needs of not only patients, but patients' families, particularly as they moved back and forth between home and hospital. But the nurses were frustrated; they wanted to know more about the families' experiences as a foundation for providing better care.

The literature provided little guidance. There was nothing that provided a way to view patients and their families that allowed practitioners to apply the best possible care in each situation. The titles of several articles indicated a family perspective. In reading the papers however, the family perspective was usually from the viewpoint of only one member, usually the spouse of the patient.

Very few studies included any other family member. Even when they did, it was most often after the patient had died. Consequently, research reports were based on recall of the palliative care situation, and excluded the patient, who of course was central to the palliative care experience in the first place. Those few studies in which data were collected before the death and included the patient were directed toward limited aspects of the experience, such as symptom management. The literature provided exhortations that the patient and family should be cared for as a unit, but provided little direction on how to actually deliver family centered care and meet that challenge. These studies were informative and helpful in guiding care; however, they did not address the whole of the family's experience.

We decided that a study focusing on the family, taking into account the limitations of other studies, would be the thrust of our first research project. Specifically, it would be prospective and would include the patient in addition to other family members. We hired a research consultant to assist us in the design of such a study, and spent several days identifying the significant variables. We identified numerous variables, some of which had been investigated or alluded to as important in other research. We then selected instruments which could measure these variables. After assessing their utility (reliability, validity, and other factors), we finalized a list of eight to ten instruments. Next, we calculated the numbers of families needed to meet the requirements for statistical calculations. We realized that the required numbers would be impossible to find within a reasonable time period. Moreover, we became concerned about approaching families who were spending the last few months, or weeks, with a loved person, and asking them to complete all these instruments. Completing a battery of instruments seemed an insensitive approach to an extremely sensitive issue.

We considered limiting the number of instruments that we would use, but regardless of the instruments we selected, we would only be capturing bits and pieces of the families' experience. Conceptually, no one theoretical model offered sufficient guidance in designing the study. There was benefit in each one we considered—coping and adaptation models, stress models, anticipatory grief models—but the selection of any one model seemed to omit other aspects which might be of relevance. We wanted a comprehensive view of what the families were experiencing. Without such an overall picture, we could not hope to appropriately guide the care that addressed the family as a unit. This view was supported by Lewis in her conclusions drawn from a critique of literature examining the impact of cancer on the family: "The predominant theoretical approach to family level research represented in the current studies needs to give way to theoretically driven investigations in order to provide a meaningful structure for measure, analysis and interpretations" [1, p. 286]. Rather than selecting a particular theoretical framework, we decided that developing a theory that derived from the families themselves was the approach we would take.

Consequently, we put aside the tools we had so methodically identified and assessed, and decided to ask the families directly about their experiences. We put aside our quantitative approach, and turned to qualitative methods which were appropriate to our question. We developed a proposal which was funded, and Phase 1 proceeded.

Meanwhile, the principle investigator, Dr. Davies, moved to Vancouver, British Columbia. Preliminary data analysis was so promising, so rich that she felt it was worth extending the study to Vancouver sites. She invited two colleagues, clinical nurse specialists employed in home-based and hospital-based palliative care programs, to participate in a parallel study (Phase 2). When data analysis was completed for both studies, and the initial conceptualization was nearly finished, Ms. Brown moved to Calgary. The completed conceptual model required verification and further elaboration; we were able to use Ms. Brown's new place of work as an additional site for this purpose (Phase 3). As a result, the study program spanned three cities in two provinces, creating a challenge to the research, and also contributing to the strength of the results. See Appendix I for details of the research process.

This book presents the results of this research program, offering a description of the experience of terminal cancer from a family perspective. The authors hope the book benefits patients with terminal cancer and their families, and helps practitioners provide optimal palliative care.

REFERENCE

1. F. M. Lewis, The Impact of Cancer on the Family: A Critical Analysis of the Research Literature, *Patient Education and Counselling, 8*, pp. 279-289, 1986.

Acknowledgments

Many people participated in the research program that resulted in this book. The idea for the research originated in the Department of Nursing, Cross Cancer Institute, Edmonton, Alberta, and included Rhea Arcand, Joy Edwards, Nola Martens, and Betty Davies. Several years, and several components later Dr. Jack Morgan was responsible for encouraging us to put the final product into this manuscript.

We are indebted to the various funding agencies that enabled us to pursue the research: the Alberta Foundation for Nursing Research, Edmonton, Alberta; the British Columbia Health Care Research Foundation, Vancouver, B.C.; and the P. A. Woodward's Foundation, Vancouver, B.C.

We thank the many individuals associated with the programs from which we recruited families for the study: the Supportive Care Program, Cross Cancer Institute, Edmonton, Alberta; the Edmonton Board of Health, Home Care Program; the Vancouver Health Department Hospice Program, Vancouver, B.C.; the Vancouver General Hospital Palliative Care Unit, Vancouver, B.C.; and the Home Care Division of Calgary Health Services, Calgary, Alberta.

Appreciation is also extended to those who assisted as research assistants and transcribers of data: Christine Gordon, Jaye Kerzner, and Jackie Warwara. Our thanks also to John Collins who was always there when we needed computer advice. Special mention goes to Brenda Austin for her editorial assistance with the manuscript, her patience with our never-ending changes, and her encouragement to send off the first draft. We are grateful to Barbara Sutherland for formatting the final draft.

We wish to acknowledge Janie Brown who wrote the chapter dealing with teenagers' experience of the transition of fading away.

To our families, we owe a special kind of gratitude. They sustained us by encouraging us and carrying on during those times when we were immersed in the research and the writing.

It seems remiss not to acknowledge how, as a group, we experienced much mirth, laughter and tears, as we worked and sustained one another through analyzing many poignant stories in the data, and through our own personal transitions of death, birth, relocation, divorce, work leave, and new relationships. The work became as much of a personal endeavor as a professional one.

Lastly, the patients and their families deserve our heartfelt thanks for intimately sharing with us a profoundly sensitive time in their living and dying. We hope that the legacy they shared with us will live on in optimal care for other families who find themselves in the transition of fading away.

Contents

Introduction

Palliative care enables people with a terminal illness to live in comfort and dignity until they die. The goal shifts from curative, life-prolonging care to the control of physical symptoms, and to psychosocial and spiritual concerns. The type of care is not an extension of accepted techniques and attitudes, but a sensitive response to the holistic needs of people whose life is coming to an end.

Quality palliative care means a shift not only in the philosophy of care but a shift in the focus of care—from the patient to the family. The entire family unit is affected when one of its members is terminally ill. Anything that affects the family system affects the individual members, just as the individual members affect the family as a whole. Good palliative care of the patient intertwines with that of the family.

Because palliative care practitioners view the family as the primary unit of care, they need a comprehensive understanding of the terminal stage of cancer as experienced by the family, including the patient. Without this, they limit their efforts to guide and support individuals through this stage. This book represents one of the first efforts to focus on the experience of the patient and family as they describe it themselves.

Much debate in family nursing, and other fields, focuses on defining the unit of care as either the patient within the context of his family or as the family as a whole. Findings from this research indicate that this debate only dichotomizes the issue. Most importantly, practitioners want to appreciate that the family as a whole has a life of its own, that is distinct, but always connected to the individuals who are part of it. Families are complex, dynamic networks of interdependent and interacting relationships. Family centered palliative care means that practitioners must address the needs of each family member, including the patient, individually, and also focus on the family as a whole. Individual and group interviews in this study yielded data which indicated that each family member has different perceptions of the situation, and has varying needs. Individual variations can be better understood when viewed within the context that the family unit is different from, but closely interrelated to, the individual lives of its members. Consequently, the following chapters address the experiences of the patients, spouses, and children separately. The final chapters look at the experience of the family as a unit. Taken together, they describe the experiences of families coping with a family member who has advanced cancer.

Once the patient and family acknowledge the terminal nature of the illness and the fact the patient will not recover, the transition of "fading away" begins, in more than just the physical sense. The transition is a process that occurs over time and includes several components that accumulate, overlap, or recur.

To set the stage, the first chapter of this book gives an overview of the fading away process and describes the trigger for its beginning. Subsequent chapters describe the components in more depth and give palliative care practitioners guidelines for care of the patient and family. Toward the end of the book, the authors explain the importance of family dynamics. And, a final chapter describes the effect of location of care on the family's terminal care experience.

The authors interviewed twenty-three families. In all families, the patient and spouse participated. In all but two families, one child participated. In two other families, two children participated. In total, seventy-one family members were in the study. Some patients had lived with cancer for as long as four years; others were diagnosed a few months before their interview. All were identified by their physician as no longer receiving curative therapies, and judged by their clinicians as people who would not be seriously burdened by the study. Although patients were all in the terminal component of cancer, the research results may have relevance for other terminal illnesses.

CHAPTER 1

Fading Away

There's been a decline in her mobility and in her bodily functions . . . her physical being is fading. Her mental capacity is fading . . .

Mr. B. referring to his wife, now bedridden

Families with a member who has terminal cancer are in transition: the transition from living with cancer to experiencing a death from cancer. During this experience, some families describe the patient as "fading away." The physiological changes limit or alter how they experience the essence of the person who is dying, and how the dying person experiences life. In other words, fading away encompasses more than the physiological changes—these are important but not sufficient to understand the experience. The physiological changes inhibit the expression of other aspects of the person.

The transition of fading away involves several components which occur over time, not necessarily in the sequence described in this book. The components include redefining, burdening, struggling with paradox, contending with change, searching for meaning, living day-to-day, and preparing for death. The components accumulate, overlap, and recur but must begin with the patient's redefinition of self and the family's redefinition of the patient. Without this, the family cannot come to terms with the other components of the fading away process. In an essential first step, the patient and family adjust or redefine their views to fit the reality of how the patient now looks and what the patient can presently do. All members of the family must adjust their view of the patient, themselves, each other, and the family as a unit.

Redefining continues throughout the experience with no clear ending, but once the family begins this process other components of the fading away process come into play. The patient confronts the possibility of being a burden and other family members confront

3

being burdened with extra responsibility. The family struggles with the paradox of the patient living with cancer but at the same time dying from cancer. All members of the family unit face major changes in their lives and search for meaning in the experiences that confront them. Toward the end of these experiences the patient and family live day-to-day and prepare for death.

The trigger for the fading away process comes when the family members recognize, separately or together, the decline in the patient's condition. They realize he or she will not recover. The patient's condition worsens in such a way that the inevitable can no longer be denied. As long as the patient maintains some sense of normalcy, or rallies (for example, going for a drive or eating more), some hope for recovery exists. The apparent normality makes it easier to believe that the patient is still all right. In the words of one daughter as she spoke about her mother, "... I can continue to deceive myself ... she tells me that it has spread, but because she continues to look good and doesn't seem much more tired ... that piece of information slides downstream."

A change in the patient's physical appearance signals a decline in the patient's condition. The patient may lose weight, become weaker, less mobile or less mentally able. However, recognition of this comes as an assault for family members: "It struck me hard;" "It was a jolt;" "It hit me ... POW! This is definitely not going to get better." The realization often comes suddenly even though there may have been clues all along. And, from this point on, family members acknowledge to themselves that the patient is, in fact, fading away.

Patients poignantly describe the changes in their own bodies: "I've shrunk a lot, not a little bit ... I have thought of myself as starting to disappear ... my nose is getting closer to my toes because of the disintegration of vertebrae and bones ..." Patients describe the decline and change in their physical appearance as being like an "Ethiopian famine victim," or "feeling eroded." As one said, "I get weaker and weaker ... I can't eat as much ... I'm fading, I know I'm fading." And another, "I'm sitting. I've sat in this living room more in the last two months than I think I have in the last two years."

Decreased mental ability presents, perhaps, the most devastating indication of decline. A woman who used to be a teacher said with emotion in her voice,

> I have loss of memory, a terrible memory for things that happened today and yesterday ... I find it really hard to do the

bank books and math. Subtracting just takes me ages, and I was
good at things like that, doing the banking and so on.

The decline in the patient's condition impacts profoundly on the
emotions of the adult children. They expect their parents will always
be vital and capable and more competent than themselves. The
patient's decline alters the image the children have of their parent
from "strong" to "frail," from "big" to "wasted." They see their parent
as incapable of handling even the smallest task and this devastates
them. "Things that were so easy for him at one time are so difficult
for him now . . . getting out of the car, having to lift his legs. And I
know he's not going to get better." And, again, "He wants to visit but
he knows he has to lie down, and if that isn't fading, I don't know
what is."

More so than spouses, the children remain sensitive to the
patient's loss of independence in personal care:

> I notice that all the things I am used to as far as social niceties
> and personal grooming habits (which) I took for granted . . .
> start to disappear, and I have to do (them) for him . . . and his
> lack of concern . . . I feel badly for him that he's lost his com-
> posure.

Although difficult, the acknowledgment that the patient will not
recover enables the patient and family members to face the challenges that lie ahead in the transition of fading away.

CHAPTER 2

Redefining

I have begun to redefine myself as someone who cannot walk alone, but I have not yet redefined myself as someone who needs a wheelchair—I can manage with a walker.

Mrs. W., age fifty
housewife and mother with cancer of the pancreas

The realization that a loved one is dying results in a major change for the entire family. This demands that family members adjust not only outwardly, but also inwardly where they keep connections to the people and places that act as definitions of self. Families need to redefine their life situation.

Redefining involves a shift in terms of what used to be and what is now and leads to an adjustment in how individuals view themselves and each other, as well as how they define the family unit. The family accommodates to changes in the patient's status through redefining and copes with the losses and gains incurred. This process goes on throughout the transition of fading away with no clear ending, and is the basis for the other components of the fading away process.

Family members' readiness to redefine the patient as different is critical to their accommodating to changes imposed by the illness. They need to relinquish former views of themselves as well as of others in the family and adjust their behavior and patterns of living. The patient's redefinition of self is the central factor in this process. When patients succeed at redefining themselves, they ease the process for others in the family. If any member of the family triad (patient, spouse, and adult child) remains unwilling to redefine the patient, this impedes redefinition for the other family members and results in resistance to changes in patterns of living. This causes tension as family members try to evade the effects of the progressing illness and act as if little has changed. Although family members

7

may redefine at different times, personal and interpersonal frustration results if disjunction persists.

PATIENTS

Redefining for patients means they let go of their view of who they used to be and develop a new view of themselves and others. Patients alter their identity over time. As their capacities become more limited, their identity narrows. They relinquish certain aspects of themselves. A man redefined his work identity in this way:

> I can't do the physical work any more. I'd like to, but I know I can't. It's the same with my job. I was a supervisor at a gas plant ... but I had to accept the fact that with the seizures I was having, I couldn't go back to that role.

As a central strategy, patients often maintain their normal patterns for as long as possible, and then implement feasible alternatives. One patient who was a teacher, brought in a stool with wheels so she could retain some mobility in her classroom. When her condition deteriorated, she took sick leave. "I had to stop with the year incomplete. That was a very hard psychological blow ... I'm just so glad I didn't have to resign at that point because it was just too hard." It was as if she were saying, "I can redefine myself as not teaching the way I used to do, but I am still a teacher." This same woman found new ways of expressing herself as her condition deteriorated. When she could not work any more, she took up watercoloring. When she could not sit any more, she began to knit while propped up in bed. When she could not do that, she read. When her vision failed, she continued to think and to explore questions in discussion with friends.

In another strategy, patients pay attention to details. One woman who could not hike any more, focused on her immediate environment: "I am more alert to the ordinary things. Now, I will often lie on the chesterfield and look out at an old wind vane ... I've never really appreciated that old wind vane and it's been there for years and years." She goes on to say, "I've thoroughly enjoyed watching the sparrows and the little ones learning to fly, and I've really had a lot more pleasure out of things like that because of having the time to do it."

In another approach, patients reinforce the fact that their internal characteristics remain the same while their physical aspects change. One patient told visitors, "I'm still D. Don't treat me any differently than you did before. My soul and my spirit are the same. People tell me my personality hasn't changed, so that's good." Another woman described the change in her spiritual identity: "I always used to think of people as the frame; I wasn't all that deep about it, about one's soul or spirit and so on. That's been a pretty major change for me. I've become much more interested in spiritual matters." Although patients talk of changes in themselves, they emphasize that they remain the same person. Their bodies change, and their capabilities change, but the essence of the person stays the same: "The physical me is no longer here as I was . . . it seems that I'm trapped in this sort of helpless little carcass. But my mind and my soul, I think, are the same."

Patients accept the limitations imposed by the disease with difficulty. They speak about their new selves with sadness and a sense of loss. They see no alternative. One patient indicated a friend's advice helped him with this acceptance:

> . . . you've got to let it go for now . . . you have to drop that . . . and if you can, at a later time, look back at it, but for right now, the way you're going through things, you have to be concerned with what's going on, and let other people do those things that you used to do.

When the patient redefines himself or herself as someone who still has accomplishments, still sees the "essence" of self, shifts in the way he or she meets the world, or discovers a different way of meeting the world, then he or she achieves reasonable contentment. Patients make the adjustments that their declining state demands. They seem to accept their situation and make the best of it. Although they redefine themselves, they differentiate those aspects which remain intact and those which have changed. They convey this to others and continue to receive support.

When patients cannot redefine themselves, they experience a sense of anger, worthlessness and frustration with the altered situation. When they recognize the changes in themselves, but do not allow these to alter their regular patterns, then they redefine themselves, but to a lesser degree. For example, Mr. M. recognized his weakness, but continued his workaholic pattern: ". . . I stuccoed part of the garage with a finished pattern. I did that Friday. It was all I could do . . . It just about killed me. I couldn't hold up anything, I was so weak. . . ."

Another patient who rigidly maintained his normal activities and self-perceptions said: "If I get worse and worse, I'll just get through it . . . I've made up my mind." He described few strategies beyond his usual pattern which put his safety at risk. ". . . every step I take is a struggle so there are times I break down, but very, very seldom." These patients experience discontent, frustration, and anger which distances others from them. They often feel abandoned, isolated, and unsupported.

The perceptions of other people affect the redefining process for patients and reinforce their perceptions of the physical changes:

> Some people get scared when they look at me. I can see it in their eyes. They don't really know quite what to say and I think they are distressed at the physical changes. It's uncomfortable to be around a person who is terribly ill.

SPOUSES

When spouses redefine the patient they acknowledge the physical changes, but take these in stride. They remain aware of the changing nature of the patient's condition. They see subtle changes daily which take away hope for recovery:

> When I get very depressed, it is usually when I am sitting here alone with him, and I see how very weak he is. I see how he falls asleep at a moment's notice . . . it's difficult to see him getting so weak when he was such a strong person before. . . . I suppose that hope is fading.

They see the changes as a result of the disease process or treatment complications, rather than a conscious decision on the part of the patient to behave in a certain way. As one husband said,

> You really have to be able to bend with the wind . . . to understand that sometimes a person's pain or reaction to a drug . . . can cause her to say or do some stupid things. But if you realize that it's really not her doing it . . . I think that you can cope with that.

Spouses rationalize patients' behavior so as to be empathetic and continue with their care. One wife said of her husband,

> Once people are ill, all their bad qualities come out but you keep on loving them because they're not doing it intentionally. I

wouldn't say he's doing this to hurt me. He's doing this because
he hurts. So, I don't hold him responsible for any of it.

The spouse often focuses on understanding the ill person's perspective of the physical changes: "We have to view her in a different way.
She's aged tremendously. She's fifty-five years old, and she's now
walking around in a body that I would attribute to a ninety-year-
old." He sees the patient's perspective of how difficult it must be in
such a body.

Redefining for spouses focuses on the relationship with the
patient. The ease with which they redefine the relationship relates
to the patient's success at redefining himself or herself. For example,
Mrs. F.'s redefinition of herself facilitated her husband's view
of their relationship as a "beautiful time in our lives." One wife
acknowledged that her husband's general weakness and fatigue
meant that "...we slowed down. And, of course, it made quite a
difference in our sexual activities too, which was traumatic to him
and he thought he was letting me down." The continuing relationship, despite the patient's physical limitations, is of importance to
the spouses: "It's really an eye opener to see how a person can adjust
to a serious illness and still continue a meaningful relationship. It's
not easy, but I don't think it's all that difficult either."

Spouses continue as normal, make adjustments as needed or consider alternatives: "We try to live as naturally as we did before ...
enjoying the same things like gardening, although P. has to stay out
of the sun right now ... so then we read together, we watch TV
together." They reorganize their priorities and put the relationship
and the comfort of the home first:

> I've put more emphasis on our close relationship. I always have
> done that, but not as close as now ... drawing together as a
> family ... rather than going my own way and doing my own
> thing and worrying about my work ...

Spouses in less favorable relationships use this strategy as well,
although the motivation differs. Mrs. M., for example, believed "you
can improve your relationship only when you're both healthy ... it's
up to the healthy one to look after the sick one."

Some spouses rely on a belief system which could be religious or
based on deeply ingrained views on the roles of marital partners in
the care of the sick. One woman said, "... we've got Bible scripture
that says 'Do all things as unto God.' So then, I'm not doing it (caring

for husband) just for him, I'm doing it for God, so it's given me a different way of still doing the same thing." Her belief allowed her to provide the care she felt was necessary because she labeled the care as "unto God" rather than "unto her husband."

When patients redefine themselves appropriately and spouses redefine their priorities, spouses feel more content, believe they support the patient and feel satisfied with their support. Some spouses feel closer to the patient and believe their relationship grows. These spouses describe their interactions with the patient not as one-sided, but reciprocal. Often this reciprocity extends to their relationships with others. One spouse said of his wife:

> It's marvellous to see that strength she is able to give to other people that come into the house to visit her. They go out of the house just shaking their heads. They can't believe that she is able to hang on and convey that love, that warmth, that openness.

When patients do not redefine themselves, spouses avoid situations that force the patient to confront the need for change. One spouse, for example, avoided tidying the household because it reminded her husband he was not able to work. "I know it upsets him, it disturbs him that he can't be a part of it, so why change it? Just leave it. Let him rest." However, the spousal relationship suffers when patients do not redefine themselves, as with Mr. N. who acknowledged he had some physical limitations but continued to define himself as a workaholic. This served to push others away and made life very hard for his wife. She saw the physical changes in him and understood his need to continue to work, but because he stubbornly clung to his former image of himself, she found the relationship trying.

When patients have difficulty redefining themselves and spouses avoid situations that demand redefinition, the spouses feel frustrated. The patient rejects their efforts of support:

> I can't even talk to him about it (his sickness) because . . . his response is, "What do you want to know for?" He can't appreciate that if he was calm and quiet about it and nice to be around, not lash out at me, I'd want to do more things for him.

These spouses try their best to "endure" the situation as a means of survival, but they do not "grow" and neither does their relationship. They become exhausted.

CHILDREN

The changes in the patient's physical condition impact profoundly on the adult children. The drastic changes require a major shift in perception of their parent from someone in control and strong to someone who is now the opposite:

> I always thought of him as, not invulnerable, but a very strong individual. And, his bout with cancer shows just how frail everybody is and he was susceptible to these things just like everyone else . . . It really made me step back and take another look at him.

Children realize that the usual life course which ends in death will be true for their parent as well.

One young man recalled his grandmother's condition before she died, and compared his father's appearance to that:

> I just remember her as very robust like my father, and her fading away and just becoming a skinny little frail old skeleton, which is how I'm seeing my father progress too. Whether that's just a natural progression of aging and death . . . I don't know . . . I haven't been around enough people in that situation.

The realization that their parent faces death means adult children redefine themselves as vulnerable. One son said, "you . . . realize how frail you are. You read the paper every day and see that people your age, early 30s and late 20s, are coming down with cancer . . . it could be me in six months' time." And another said, "I've let my health slip a little bit in the last couple of years. Now I'm concentrating on getting that back." Their parents' earlier advice sometimes reinforces this resolution: "Your health and your time are precious. Don't waste them."

Part of redefining for the children involves facing the future without the parent. Children talk explicitly about their visions of this, in particular, about their parent never being a grandparent: "When I do get around to having a family, there will be no memory there (of my father) for my sons and daughters. That hurts." However, when children think of the parent not only as a physical being but as living in memories or legacies, this helps redefine their future without the parent. One adult child remembered a fitting quote: "The soul of the dead lives on in the memories of the living."

As a strategy to redefine their parent, children try to view the evident changes as a result of the illness or treatment instead of intentional behavior: "I look at his behaviour (hallucinating) and realize that it's not my father that is doing this consciously. This is something that he no longer has any control over . . ." Children also recognize the attributes of the parent that continue despite the fact the parent is failing: "He gets more tired, and he feels (life) slipping away, but he's always had a strong will."

Adult children come to recognize the situation as beyond their personal control: "A guy can sit and rationalize and say that you know he is slipping away, and there isn't much you can do about it, and come to grips with that." Frustration and anger accompany redefining when the patient had not sought help early enough for his or her symptoms. To address this, children attempt to understand the behavior in the context of how the parents had always been. Again, they recognize the situation as beyond their control:

> I couldn't come out and say to him, ". . . I think you should go and have a really good exam because I think you have (cancer) . . ." it was certainly gentle prodding but it didn't get me very far, and that's just the way my parents have been. They have never been active in their care and have never sought a lot of help.

In a strategy for managing their parent's loss of social niceties, grooming habits, and change in mental state, children discourage visitors and redefine the situation as a private experience open only to the family: "It's a protective thing because I don't think it's appropriate and I wouldn't want them (friends of the children) to see Dad like that . . . it's not very dignified for him . . ."

As a result of redefining, children acknowledge death is a part of life and recognize they have limitations in its control. They realize their own susceptibility to illness and death and that of the people they love. They resolve to take better care of themselves.

In contrast to successful redefinition, some adult children may continue as if nothing had changed and try to recreate the past without its hurtful moments. These children devote all of their attention on the relationship with the patient and on creating a "perfect family," which causes tension and conflict within the family. In so doing, they neglect their family of procreation.

GUIDELINES FOR CARE

A sensitive practitioner appreciates that a family's reluctance to relinquish old and comfortable views of themselves for new and unfamiliar ones is related to their fears about suffering and death. The disengagement from former views, redefinition of the situation and adoption of new orientations all occur over time. The conundrum for the practitioner centers on anticipating and preparing family members for what lies ahead without violating their need to relinquish old orientations and hopes at a pace they can handle. The fact that redefining does not necessarily occur simultaneously with physical changes in the patient or with information that people are given about the escalation of the illness, makes this even more difficult.

While patients redefine themselves, family members also redefine the patients, their relationships with one another, and interactions within the family. Because different people redefine themselves in several different realms, these redefinitions may not be congruent. The practitioner tailors interventions according to the various abilities of family members to assimilate the changes. At the same time, however, the practitioner supports the family as a unit. One way the practitioner accomplishes this is by normalization— reassuring family members that a range of responses and coping strategies is to be expected.

Practitioners will find the following guidelines helpful in caring for patients, spouses, and adult children. The guidelines derived from the direct accounts of the patients, spouses, and children about the strategies they used to cope. However, many of the guidelines may be appropriate for other family members. For example, the guidelines suggesting that spouses have opportunities to talk about changes in their relationship with the patient could also apply to other family members, as they, too, experience changes in their relationships. However, it was the spouses in the study who particularly emphasized this aspect. Consequently, this guideline was directed to spouses. Practitioners need to use their clinical judgment in applying the guidelines to other family members.

Patients

- Provide opportunities for patients to talk about the losses incurred by the illness, the enforced changes, the adaptations they made and their feelings associated with these.

- Reinforce normal patterns of living as long as possible and as appropriate.
- Focus on what patients can still do. Review alternatives when patients can no longer function as they did. Suggest they undertake parts of their previous activities or approach these differently rather than abandon them.
- Reinforce those aspects of self that remain intact. Acknowledge that roles and responsibilities may be expressed differently. For example, the role of mother may be expressed through physical presence and verbal guidance for the children as opposed to physical help.
- Suggest new activities, appropriate to the patient's interest and current capabilities.

Spouses

- Explain how the disease or treatment contributes to changes in the patient physically, psychologically, and socially.
- Provide opportunities for spouses to talk about how changes in the patient affect their marital relationship.
- Reinforce normal patterns of living as long as possible and appropriate.
- Focus on the patient's attributes that remain intact. Acknowledge that these may be expressed differently as, for example, in the role of mother described previously.
- Consider adjustments or alternatives when former patterns are no longer feasible, such as using a wheelchair to go for a walk in the park.
- Provide opportunities for spouses to discuss how they may reorganize priorities in order to be with and care for the patient to the degree they desire. Consider resources that enable the spouse to do this, such as volunteers, home support services, or additional nursing services. Teach caregiving techniques, if the spouse shows interest.

Children

- Explain how the disease or treatment contribute to changes in the patient physically, psychologically, and socially.
- Focus on the patient's positive aspects that remain intact, even if expressed differently.

- Help children appreciate the parent from another perspective, for example, in memories acquired and legacies left.
- Discuss how children can face their own vulnerability by channeling concerns into positive steps for self care.
- Discuss the degree to which children wish to be open or private about the patient's illness with those outside the family.
- Acknowledge that family members will vary in their ability to assimilate changes in the patient and in family life, and that a range of responses and coping strategies will emerge as family members cope as best they can.

CHAPTER 3

Burdening

I'm pretty well stuck right here, but my wife should have some kind of outlet . . . because it must be just like being in a prison in a way.

Mr. C., age sixty-five
cancer of prostrate with spinal metastasis

In the fading away process, patients may think they burden others, and spouses and children may feel burdened. Burdening has many facets. Patients feel they are a burden because of the extra work they create. Spouses acknowledge the additional demands they assume, but do not describe the additional load as burdensome. Adult children have mixed feelings about incorporating the extra responsibilities into their already busy lives.

Patients think they burden others and express concern when they require others to assume their personal care or take on their former roles. They believe they burden their families because they "hold them up." "I can tell that everyone's life has changed on account of this . . . they can't get on with their lives." They perceive family members as overloaded with responsibilities when they search for appropriate foods, give pain medications during night hours, or manage bowel and bladder problems. The sense of burden worsens when patients see themselves as purposeless, dependent, unable to get around:

> I had to deal with suddenly becoming so dependent . . . a big change here is that someone who is twenty-two-years-old is having to look after me . . . When she first came, I was the one looking after her and her new baby.

Patients believe themselves a burden to the degree to which they have not constructively redefined themselves. When they do redefine themselves, they use their limited energy for emotional support and encouragement as a way of easing the burden for family members. For example, Mrs. F. acknowledged the additional responsibilities her husband assumed and assisted him as much as she could by appreciating his efforts and acknowledging his concerns: "I'm trying just to relate a lot . . . I know he's really worried but he doesn't say much about how he feels, but lately, we've been talking more realistically and it's better for both of us, much better."

Patients use several strategies in an attempt to alleviate their sense of burden. Often, they avoid complaint: "There's no way I would want to put any greater burden on them . . . by moaning and groaning and crying about the situation." Sometimes, they select with whom they share their concerns and worries:

> I can talk with my husband the best about what I am experiencing and going through, and I don't really like to talk to my kids too much about it. . . . I don't want to dwell on it with them. With them, I want to know what's happening in their lives.

In another approach, patients encourage or give permission to family members to go out and continue with life: "I tell my kids that I want them to go and enjoy their lives, not to worry so much about me, but they're always concerned." One man encouraged his wife to continue to go out, just to get out of the house.

Patients utilize the skills and strengths they retain to do as much as possible while they are able and to be useful to other family members. One woman, on the days she had a little more energy, swept the floor and left the pile of dust for her husband to pick up. A man who used to be the family mechanic, advised his children on how to care for the car when he could no longer do it himself.

Some patients accept and prepare for death as a strategy to relieve the burden on their families: "I know I'm dying and I'm not afraid. I'd rather go sooner than later because it's hard on the family." When patients implement strategies such as these, they contribute, although in a different way, and relieve their sense of burden. When they limit their demands and complaints as much as possible, family members feel more willing to provide the necessary care.

When patients do not redefine themselves or perceive themselves as a burden, they use their energy to maintain their former view of themselves, often at the expense of the spouse-caregiver. Patients minimize or deny the strain on family members and have no energy to support them emotionally. Patients underestimate the demands they place on others; consequently, their care lacks some compassion and affection. For example, Mr. P., said, "I can't do anything. It's a burden on my wife, but I do a bit yet . . . sure, there's some extra work for her, but I don't think it's all that much." Mr. P. does not think he burdens his wife, nor does he acknowledge her efforts. However, from her perspective, he is very demanding and requires considerable physical assistance. She thinks he does not consider her feelings at all.

SPOUSES

While spouses acknowledge their extra roles and responsibilities, many hesitate to describe them as a burden. Rather, they describe them as necessary when someone you love is ill and needs care. When spouses believe the patient acknowledges and appreciates their efforts, they are even less likely to feel burdened. One husband, who assumed many of the household chores and did much of his wife's personal care, did not indicate he felt burdened at all. In fact, he stated, "She gives as much back to me as I give to her."

Spouses recognize the patients' concerns about burden and, as a primary strategy, offset their worries with reassurances. When one wife regretted her inability to do work in the house, her spouse said: "Well, you're supposed to sit still, rest, and get well." In another approach, spouses revise their personal priorities for a balance between caregiving and self-care: "I've let things go that I don't feel are as important right now, so we're balancing our life quite easily that way." These spouses do not experience caregiver burden and report a sense of satisfaction in what they do for the patient.

However, spouses who experience burden exhibit a sense of waiting for the patient to die. Death will lift the burden and the spouse can then attend to all that has been put on hold. These spouses feel exhausted and their own health deteriorates. One spouse who assumed personal care for the patient, and did all the household chores, felt her husband did not appreciate her efforts and wearily and repeatedly said, "It's a load, it's a load." Such feelings of burden occur when patients do not redefine themselves and persist in their usual lifestyle. They do not recognize the impact on family caregivers. Mr. R., for example, wanted to keep his many pets but was unable to care for them. His wife said, ". . . everything is my responsibility. He doesn't hear the animals in the night . . . I'm up two or three times a night. He brought home strays and that's why we have all these animals . . . it makes work."

Spouses who acknowledge a sense of burden, use several coping strategies. First, they rationalize their situation by simply "keeping going" or "doing what you have to do," and finding comfort in that. Mrs. R. coped by turning to her religious belief that "We are all God's people . . . every life is God's life . . . it belongs to Him, and, therefore, I ask what can I do to help this one." Second, and this relates to the first, they put their own needs on hold while they try to please the patient. In a final strategy, they acknowledge the burden will be lifted when the patient dies: "I'll be fine, I'm sure, after (he dies) because a heavy, heavy weight will be lifted off my shoulders."

The two groups of spouses differ in that the first willingly give and value the extra time spent with the patient while the second feels obligated to spend the extra time with the patient and feels deprived of the time for other activities.

CHILDREN

Similar to spouses, adult children assume extra work and responsibilities. However, this superimposes on the demands of their careers, of their own children and of the home. For example:

> Because we have a commitment to our animals, by the time we get home, get dinner, go to Mom and Dad's house, and come back here, it's usually ten o'clock at night . . . both of us just seem to be dragging ourselves around . . . Some days you just really feel like packing it all in . . . but who else is going to do it?

In contrast to the spouses, who either feel they get some satisfaction out of caring for the patient or feel burdened, children have mixed feelings. They feel exhausted on the one hand, and on the other, satisfied with their contribution.

The health of the well parent acts as a major intervening factor in the degree of burden for adult children. If the spouse remains well and able to care for the ill parent, then the stress on the children relates to support of that parent and concern for his or her future welfare after the death of the spouse. When the well parent cannot adequately care for the spouse or him/herself, then the children experience greater stress. In one situation, the adult children believed the wife did not respond appropriately to her husband's condition and could not care for him or his business. As a result, the son and daughter-in-law experienced a greater sense of burden. In another family, the children worried about the spouse's ability to care for herself: "... this really has taken a big toll on Mom and we're seeing some changes in her. She's not eating well, so we bring her meals that we have prepared." Children cope with their concerns for the welfare of the caregiving parent in a number of ways. They keep in touch, inform the parent of their whereabouts, visit as often as possible, and oversee their parent's health. When the well parent functions poorly, the children spend more time with the parent, encouraging, teaching, and helping.

Adult children reorganize their priorities as a strategy to handle the sense of burden. In this way they maintain the level of support they want to and gain a sense of satisfaction. They decrease their recreation, social, and rest time. In some families, children share the extra duties by distributing the tasks among the members of the sibling group. They cope with the competing demands on their time by reminding themselves of the importance of the extra time spent with their parent. Adult children also take time out for themselves as a strategy to handle burden. They sometimes talk with or seek support from friends which provides relief and distraction from the persistent stress.

When children cannot reorganize their priorities or take time for themselves, an overwhelming sense of exhaustion sets in. The children want it to be over, one way or another. In an attempt to alleviate the parents' perception of burden, children reassure the patient, and the well parent, that they are not burdens for them. In response to his father's advice, "Go and enjoy your life, don't worry so much about me," one young man replied,

> I do spend a lot of time with mom and dad . . . and they feel they may be holding me up, but I don't feel that way. I want to spend time with them. They are telling me to get on with my own life, but I'm not ready for that right now.

GUIDELINES FOR CARE

Practitioners help patients find ways to relieve the sense of burden. They also help spouses and adult children understand the patient's need to stay involved for as long as possible as a way to sustain self-esteem and a sense of control. Practitioners assist family members to take on tasks appropriate to their comfort level and skill, share tasks among themselves, and plan for respite time from the outset. This avoids a sense of burden or resentment for one or two family members and legitimizes respite time, which then enables families to provide care and support over time and avoid exhaustion.

Patients

- Provide opportunities for patients to talk about fears and anxieties of dying and death. In addition, recommend a listener from a volunteer program or support group. Recommend helpful books or pamphlets for the patient, such as those from local hospice groups or cancer agencies.
- Provide opportunities for patients to consider with whom to share their concerns and worries. In this way, they need not place excessive demands on certain family members.
- Explain the importance of a break for family members and suggest patients accept help from a volunteer or home support services at those times to relieve the family of worry. When patients encourage other members to take breaks, they reciprocate the concern they receive from their family.
- Encourage patients to participate in day-to-day activities as appropriate, even if this involves parts of activities. Help them recognize new approaches, such as teaching others what they formerly would have done for them.
- Explain that when patients affirm family members for their efforts, this contributes to their feeling appreciated and reduces feelings of burden.
- Appreciate that for some patients, accepting and being ready for death is their way of relieving burden for others.

Spouses

- Support the spouse's reassurances to the patient that he or she is not a burden.
- Acknowledge spouses for their efforts when they put their own needs on hold to care for the patient. Help them to appreciate that they must still take care of themselves as a legitimate way to sustain the energy they need for the patient.
- Consider how spouses may take some time out. Review resources such as home support services or volunteers who provide respite time for the spouse.

- Acknowledge the negative feelings spouses may have about how long they can continue; do not negate the positive desires they feel to help.

Children

- Acknowledge the reorganization of priorities and the considerable adjustment in daily routines. Explain that the positive feelings associated with helping, as well as the negative feelings associated with less time spent on careers and family, contribute to their feelings of ambivalence and strain.
- Anticipate the demands for patient care that lie ahead and assist children to identify their priorities in preparation.
- Affirm adult children for their efforts in adjusting their usual routines to accommodate the extra demands.
- Acknowledge that when they keep in touch, visit more often and stay available by phone, this all represents the "work" of caring and should not be underestimated.
- Encourage children to take time out for themselves, especially to socialize or gain support by talking with understanding friends.

CHAPTER 4

Struggling with Paradox

All of a sudden, your life is not finished, but you can't really think ahead.

Mr. O., age forty-four
cancer of bowel with metastases to lung and brain

During the process of fading away, the patient struggles with the paradox of living with cancer and at the same time dying from cancer. Wanting to spend time with and care for their spouse while continuing with the on-going requirements of daily life is the primary paradox for spouses. Children experience several paradoxes related to the complexities of caring for ill parents while fulfilling responsibilities for their own careers and families.

PATIENTS

The dilemma of "I'm going to live," versus "I'm not going to live," reflects the central paradox for patients. One woman said, "My husband was told that my time was pretty limited, and I was thinking, 'That's ridiculous. I'm going to live for a long time yet' . . . the fact is that I very likely won't make it."

The patient's desire to fight, to keep going, vies with the desire to give up: "You don't want to leave this world . . . but you sometimes wonder what's the point of staying around." If the patient stays alive he or she suffers. As one woman said: "There are times when I would just like to go to sleep. . . . and, other times, when I really want to fight."

Patients frequently acknowledge the up and down nature of the disease which affects the struggle. One person explained the process:

I wonder, . . . as I'm supposedly in such a bad way, why I get these times when I can eat and I'm hungry and I wake up and I feel there's quite a bit of energy, and I want to do things, and yet I can't. I guess that must be the nature of the disease as it waxes and wanes.

When patients feel good, they hope they live and when they do not feel so good, they acknowledge they probably will not make it.

Some people struggle with how active they should be in treatment, either with supportive therapies such as nutritional supplements, or with medical treatment directed at controlling the cancer symptoms. They wonder whether to try different approaches to put up the best fight, or to accept the situation as it is and "let go."

I certainly have thought of giving up on the pills and all the vitamins and supplements and maybe not eating as much. But, that would be a form of suicide, and I can't do that. And I don't want a lot of pain, and I don't want resuscitation . . . so, we are of two minds, still. On the one hand, it's not going to do much good to have any more treatment, but then, on the other hand, it will relieve pain for awhile . . . And, then every once in a while, we think that maybe a miracle will happen.

And again:

I'm in limbo . . . Can I do something to help? I don't know . . . Should I go on the carotene treatment? Will it help? I guess the specialists have got to know about that. If they thought there was a better solution . . . they would be advising people. So, I guess I feel I'm getting the best treatment or information that's available to me . . . but I still feel I should be doing something.

Despite their acknowledgment of the poor prognosis, patients often hold out hope that they might experience a miracle, a remission. For example: "I'm still very hopeful that there will be a miracle and somehow I'll beat it." And, again, "I keep wishing for something that would arrest it a bit." At the very least many hope for life after death.

Some patients fight for the sake of their families: "If I didn't have any family . . . I think I'd just curl up and wait. Because of the family, I tend to fight." Another man said, "I don't think I could give up, just because of my family and the support I've had from them, and how much I love them."

Some patients put the dilemma out of their minds: "I know that I've got a great deal of cancer, and for most of the time, I've been able to put it out of my mind, but not lately." The man who wondered about alternative treatments eventually decided his physician would have recommended these if he thought they would be helpful and he put the paradox aside. When patients put the disease out of their minds, they facilitate interaction with others on different topics than the disease. However, this only works when they do not have pain as a constant reminder of the ongoing dilemma.

Patients focus on the good days and do as much as they can. Distractions serve a useful purpose. Having visitors enables them to focus on the activities of others. Patients keep busy, read, and concentrate on what they can accomplish rather than on their decreasing abilities. Strategies such as these enable them to tolerate the paradox. They reflect on the paradox and arrive at a decision that allows them to put it to rest, at least temporarily. They then focus on the more enjoyable aspects of their lives.

SPOUSES

Although patients often talk spontaneously about the paradox of their situation, most spouses do not experience the same dilemma. They find the struggle more relevant to patients. One husband acknowledged that his wife might want to give up: "Although she hasn't expressed this, I think that physically she is saying, 'How much more do I have to put up with?' " Spouses believe patients have the right to make their own decisions, and resign themselves to accept these:

> If my wife says, "I don't want any more pills other than pain pills. I don't want to take any fluid, or whatever," that would be her decision . . . But, she has to make that decision. I can't, and I would never, (but) I would support her decision.

Spouses, however, struggle with one paradox specific to their situation: they want to care for and spend time with the mate who is dying but they also need to continue with the day-to-day requirements of "normal" life. This results in a constant juggling of time and responsibilities:

> We try to spend as much time together as possible, but that's not realistic either, because there are some times when I want to get out and play squash or racquetball with my friends, or get out into the yard. So, I'm torn . . . I want to be upstairs with her, but I realize I have a need too, that I can't be there all the time.

Most spouses respond to this by putting aside their own needs and activities for the sake of the patient. In this way they fulfill their obligations to the patient, but when they neglect their own physical symptoms their health suffers. A few cope with the paradox by acknowledging their need to get away from the situation. They participate in outside activities and put aside feelings of guilt. These spouses reaffirm that for optimal care of their loved one, they too need some attention. They generally seem more rested and contented and do not report health problems, fatigue, or exhaustion.

The strategies spouses use to cope with paradoxes resemble those used by children to cope with burdening. In other words, different family members demonstrate the same behaviors for different reasons.

CHILDREN

Children struggle with three major paradoxes. The most important is the struggle between hanging on and letting go. They want their parent to live, but by staying alive, the parent suffers. One child said,

> There's been a real tug-of-war . . . on one hand, I want someone to do something, find a cure . . . on the other hand, the very frustrating knowledge that there is no cure . . . it would be so much better if he just died, and released his own pain, his own agony.

This dilemma tires the children and they report decreased abilities to concentrate or focus on other aspects of their lives.

Children sometimes face this paradox by putting their parent's life into perspective:

> I've tried to have a good outlook. I know things aren't good, they're not going to get any better. But I try to think Dad's had a pretty good life up till now, and life does have to go on.

They acknowledge their parent is going to die which enables them to see a balance in what appears to be an overwhelmingly negative situation. Children recognize their parents are suffering and that the suffering will only worsen if they do not die.

Sometimes adult children examine their own behavior and ask themselves: "Should I really be hanging on to him?" They change the focus from the pain they will feel when their parent dies, to the suffering the parent experiences by not dying. They change from wishing the parent would stay alive to hoping that "it happens really fast."

Children want to spend as much time with the parent as possible but want to get on with their own lives, too, and this represents the second major dilemma. This especially holds true for adolescents and young adults who face major developmental tasks of forming intimate relationships and maintaining relationships with their peer group. One young man acknowledged that his desire for a girlfriend took second place to his concerns about his father's pending death: "I'm . . . looking for a relationship right now, and Dad's situation hasn't been helping. I . . . don't want to start one with the problems I'm having right now."

These children use the energy that might ordinarily go into dating and developing personal relationships into caring for their parents. They put certain aspects of their lives on hold. One young man noted that his sadness affected his friends. "I don't like putting stress on them, so I don't usually show my true feelings in front of my friends."

However, when children do let go of their emotions and openly express frustration and sadness, this can be an effective coping strategy: "I don't often cry . . . maybe to a degree, I do hold things in, and that's not good for me, but I let it out when I can." When children express their feelings, they direct their energy to facing the situation again, rather than to hiding their feelings.

In the third major paradox, adult children with families of their own, struggle with the need to spend time with their ill parent and with their own families. They struggle with arrangements for the children's activities: they think the child should spend time with his or her grandparent while it is still possible, and they also think the child needs to continue with normal age-appropriate activities.

> Sometimes I think they're (her own sons) very selfish because they could make more time to go down and see Mum and Dad . . . but they're twenty-one and nineteen and they're going to school and they both work part-time and they're both interested in hockey . . . so their time is limited.

In coping with the paradox of dual loyalties and demands, adult children devote much energy to weighing the pros and cons of each alternative. Many change their expectations of their own children and their own spouses. For example, one woman expected her own family to take on some of the household tasks so that she could spend more time with her own mother. Others just work harder and faster and longer, trying to "do it all" and have no time for themselves.

For some children, particularly adolescents, the paradox relates to sharing information, particularly in families that limit communication about illness and the prognosis. One daughter said, "It's like wanting to know, but not wanting to ask, because that will bring the full details into their mind, maybe causing them (the parents) more pain." The parents in this family protected their children from detailed information about the patient's condition, and this lead to uncertainty. The child wondered how to communicate with the parents. Children do not face this paradox when their parents remain open with them.

GUIDELINES FOR CARE

Caring for families who are struggling with paradox involves some difficult challenges. A family's ultimate challenge is to face the usual business of living while caring for a dying family member. The practitioner's challenge is to appreciate that he/she cannot completely alleviate the psycho-social-spiritual pain inherent in a family's struggle. Ultimately, the family must come to terms with the changes and the feelings associated with them. Thus, practitioners must assess their own comfort level in working with people facing paradoxical situations and ambivalent feelings. Practitioners, like families, may want to resist the turmoil of this component. They may feel unprepared to handle conversations where no simple solution exists and where strong feelings abound. Practitioners must know themselves and their own abilities to face paradoxical, ambiguous situations.

Patients

- Provide opportunities for patients to mourn the loss of previous hopes and plans.
- Do not minimize the pain associated with patients' losses, but review those aspects of their personality, activities or roles they retain. Explain how they may express these differently and still contribute to family life. Help patients modify previous hopes and plans and consider new ones.
- Explain the normality of the up and down course of the disease. Encourage patients to make the most of their better days.

- Review sources of distraction that divert patients from thoughts of the illness and encourage them to utilize these.
- Ensure effective symptom control as this enables the patient to focus outside the illness.

Spouses

- Acknowledge that when spouses put aside their own needs, this forms part of the "work" of caring and should be appreciated as such.
- Explain the importance of respite in the context of a renewal of energy to care for the patient. Consider the need for additional resources so spouses can obtain some time out.
- Explain that people often feel guilty about taking time out, but care of self enables them to maintain caring for the patient over time.

Children

- Without minimizing the pain associated with the loss of their parent, explain that illness and death are part of the natural cycle of life. Acknowledge that although this may be inherently understood, people often feel unprepared for death and how to handle it.
- Help children consider the patient's suffering from another perspective . . . "letting go" of suffering rather than "hanging on" to life despite the suffering.
- Provide opportunities for children to ventilate their sadness and frustration.
- Explain that they may need to reduce their expectations of themselves in the care of their family of procreation to cope with patient care. Explain that this protects them from exhaustion.
- Acknowledge that when they put aspects of their own life on hold, this should not be minimized but recognized as part of the work of caring. Explain that conflicting feelings of wanting to help while resenting the extra demands are normal, given the situation.

CHAPTER 5

Contending with Change

We have no way of planning our lives—it sort of goes up and down, up and down . . . we have no way of knowing what's going to happen next.

S., daughter, whose father is gravely ill

The ill person as well as the other family members face major changes in relationships, roles, responsibilities, and social life.

PATIENTS

Patients recognize their limited time and devote more time and energy to the important people in their lives. They reexamine patterns of family interaction and consider ways they can alter their behavior. As one woman said,

> What it has given me is an opportunity to mend some fences . . . especially with my son . . . I think it has improved relationships with everybody and it made me really stop and appreciate all my friends . . . I realized that in the past eleven years I had made my son feel like a second class citizen, so one of the first things I did was to change my will, and to put him in as the executor of the estate. And, our relationship has improved tremendously, and the relationship between my daughter and my son has improved as well.

As a way of maintaining relationships, patients deliberately initiate conversation about events other than their illness. One woman said,

> I found a little while ago that I didn't have anything to say, and he's a quiet person . . . but now we're talking a bit more . . . when the TV is on, I put the mute on during the ads and we talk then . . .

Patients experience changes in their sexual relationships. One woman stated, ". . . it hurt so much to have any pressure on my bones that it was really hard on our love life . . . we both really miss each other."

Socialization with friends and family alter as patients become less able to go out of the house, and when they do, less able to participate actively. One woman stated,

> I'd plan the things we'd do and invite people over . . . but I can't really do that much now and I certainly miss going out with him (husband) to things like concerts and operas. Then you knew there would be lots to talk about.

However, when patients encourage family members to continue their participation in outside activities they can appreciate vicariously what those around them do. For example:

> I have probably been very fortunate with the number of visitors . . . they always tell me about the Al-Anon meetings and what have you . . . and friends tell me where the club is hiking every week. I find this keeps me interested.

The illness forces changes for patients in work roles, responsibilities, and household tasks. As a coping strategy they break down larger tasks into smaller ones, relinquish the difficult and retain the easy ones. One patient gave up her teaching career but described how she developed techniques for the students to be more considerate of her situation and cooperate with her. She subsequently had to relinquish other aspects of her daily life such as shopping, banking, caring for the home, and entertaining.

To cope with being housebound or even bed-bound, patients notice their environment more, such as the weather vane moving in the wind, and in particular, aspects of nature, such as the sparrows that build their nest outside the window.

Through such strategies patients experience a greater degree of contentment and recognize they handle a very difficult situation as best they can. As patients accommodate to their situation, family members and friends find it easier to respond to them and closer, more satisfying relationships result.

SPOUSES

Some spouses report their relationship with the patient grows as a result of the illness. One spouse stated, "Certainly your life has changed because of the illness but our relationship is growing and blossoming even further." They attribute changes in their sexual relationships to the physical decline of the patient:

> Our personal relationship has changed because of her illness . . . because of the severity of her illness and the rapid decline in her mobility and her bodily functions and the pain that she is in, we have to adjust to all of those things.

In contrast, other spouses describe their relationship as strained. Where members of a spousal pair previously filled their lives with separate activities, the illness enforces togetherness, and creates disharmony. For example, one woman complained, "Regardless of your differences, when you are a married couple, you do get along as two separate people. . . . He goes to work and you go your way and you're apart, but now we're here all the time."

Changes in roles and responsibilities range from personal care and emotional support for the patient to financial management and maintenance of the home:

> I think I've become a much stronger person. I always depended on my husband for an awful lot of things and now I realize that it is my turn to be strong. So, I've taken over that role.

Emotional support sometimes includes absorbing the patient's frustration with the situation. For example: "He takes it out on me because I'm the only one here and the one nearest to him." And in practical terms, another spouse stated: "All the bills and expenses and everything else were always taken care of. I'm finding it quite different to look after things myself."

Spouses reassign their personal priorities to manage the change in roles and responsibilities. They focus on the relationship:

> My priorities have changed. I've put more emphasis on our close relationship . . . and drawing together as a family rather than going my own way, doing my own things and worrying about my work. My priority now is to take care of my husband and our home, and make it as pleasant as possible for him.

Most spouses contend with change by keeping things as normal as possible within the limitations imposed by the disease. They include the patient in the usual family activities in different ways. They may put the patient's bed in a central part of the house, or place the Christmas tree in the patient's room, for instance.

Social activities diminish primarily because the patient cannot go out or entertain as much. The activities have to be less physically oriented. Spouses do not go to dances or play golf. They miss the spontaneity, the shared activities and the opportunity to talk about these afterwards. Spouses also notice less time for themselves and their normal activities: "I'd like to go out ... I would have liked to have gone out to the lake by now, and open up the cabin and hook up the water, and of course, we can't do that." Another spouse said, "I swam three times a week but since he had the operation, it's all gone. I don't walk, I don't swim, I don't do enough exercise."

In contending with change, very few spouses pay attention to their need for self care, although some patients encourage them to do so: "My wife is really good at avoiding statements like 'You're not spending enough time' ... so, I'm very fortunate to have the ability to come and go." When patients do encourage this, spouses have a greater sense of freedom, are less weary, and feel appreciated by the patients. Conversely, when spouses sacrifice their social life and their own needs for the sake of the patient's wellbeing they may neglect to prepare meals for themselves, to visit the doctor for health problems, or to seek social outings. Fatigue takes its toll.

CHILDREN

Children also describe changes in relationships, roles and socialization, but these changes are more widespread and all-encompassing. This may be due to their stage of development. Interactions with their parents, their families of procreation, and siblings alter dramatically. The changes stem from their perception of the ill parent as more vulnerable and weaker. They perceive the well parent as very stressed, not attending to self-care and needing emotional support. The children feel they now parent their parents. One son stated, "Dad was her rock. She leaned on Dad, and so now she is leaning on me more."

As a coping strategy children avoid discussions or behavior which would add to an already stressful situation:

> I tend to be highly opinionated at times and there's enough stress around so I avoid pointless arguments and conversations ... rather than fight and argue, I will let her say whatever she is saying ... it's like water off a duck's back. I feel we're getting along a little better ... me and my Dad are a lot alike so we argue a lot and we haven't been doing that as much.

In another strategy, children demonstrate for the parent's benefit that they can handle the situation. Interacting in this way does not preclude emotional closeness between the child and the parent:

> I very rarely show emotion. I feel that he's being strong so why can't I? If he sees me breaking down, what's that going to do for him? And, if I feel that I have to break down, I can. I don't have to do it in front of him.

Adult children face specific role changes—they assume responsibility for financial and legal support as well as emotional and physical care for the parents. One son reported the way he and his parents changed roles. The parents said, "Here's our income tax; it's all in the briefcase; it's yours." And the son's wife said: "My role with Dad changed a lot, from being his daughter-in-law to teaching his ostomy care . . . he feels comfortable being dependent on me . . . but I feel really uncomfortable."

When children take on such responsibilities for their parents they sacrifice their own time. This ranges from a weekly visit to several visits a week, to quitting work and spending all their time with the parents. In some families, the adult siblings coordinate what needs to be done for the parents and by whom, so they share the additional responsibilities.

Because of the amount of time spent with their parents, adult children have less time to devote to their families of procreation. Mothers, for example, cannot be at home to make meals and carry out the regular household activities. As one said: ". . . they're having to manage without me which initially was just an absolute disaster, but now they get it together and they don't have to phone me five hundred and fifty times when I'm at Mom's." However, this sometimes strains the relationship between the adult children and their families.

Changes in interactions with adult siblings center around the care of the patients and decision-making related to the management of the patients when very ill. One daughter-in-law, after a difficult time bringing together all the siblings, tried to prepare them:

> . . . but people just aren't ready to hear that. Everybody was trying to avoid it . . . there's a feeling that you have got to accept reality . . . this is what it is . . . he's dying of cancer, and he's going to go very soon.

Adult children put their social life on hold as a strategy for coping with a lack of time. When adult children do socialize they describe less spontaneity. They must deliberately plan leisure time and they rarely do so and usually only if the situation is under control. One daughter said, "Because it's very easy to get into a routine where you feel responsible for everyone and everyone's problems . . . every once in a while, I'll just make myself go out for dinner, if I know that things are fine."

The limited social activity for unmarried adult children precludes developing intimate relationships or relationships with peers. Some children find this an acceptable choice:

> The simple fact of the matter is that my work schedule does not allow a lot of free-time during the weekends, and during the week, there's not a whole lot to do, so I do spend a lot of time with my parents. They may feel they are holding me up, but I don't feel that way.

Others find the limited opportunities for social activities less acceptable:

> My Mom is a demanding person, so she expects us to be here all the time even though she says she doesn't. I know she does. Sometimes it gets hard. On my days off I feel obliged to come for a longer period of time, and I guess my life is just centered around looking after and spending time with my mother.

As a result of all the changes, many children become chronically fatigued. The amount of weariness relates to the degree of sickness of the ill parent, how much the well parent can do, the nature of their other responsibilities and the other resources available to the family. Despite the increased workload, most children get some sense of satisfaction from believing that they are doing as much as they can.

GUIDELINES FOR CARE

Practitioners have several approaches available as they support families contending with change. In one approach they create an environment in which families explore and manage their own concerns and feelings. In this way, families manage their situation in a manner that reflects their particular coping style and their past experience with loss, illness, or death. Thus, the help practitioners offer does not necessarily entail an answer or a specific solution for the family. Rather, practitioners encourage dialogue about the family members' beliefs, feelings, fears, hopes, and dilemmas so they can determine their own course of action. Practitioners strive for as much open communication as the family can handle. However, practitioners also recognize that families communicate in well-entrenched patterns and that their ability to communicate openly and honestly differs.

In a second approach, practitioners normalize the experience of family members. For example, family members may experience concern and caring toward the patient as well as anger and resentment at the extra demands. Practitioners validate these feelings as normal given the situation and explain that they do not negate the positive feelings of concern and affection.

In a third approach practitioners provide information so families can explore the available resources, their options, and the pros and cons of the various alternatives. Knowing their resources and possible choices, families are in a better position to determine what adjustments they can make.

Patients

- Assist patients to explore new approaches to communication when they have identified trouble spots in relationships.
- Help patients break down former roles and activities into smaller aspects as opposed to relinquishing the entire role or activity.
- Encourage patients to support family members' participation in activities outside the home. Explain he or she can benefit vicariously through discussion and thus share in the activities.
- Discuss how changes in position or improved pain management helps maintain sexual intimacy.

Spouses

- Acknowledge the wide-ranging nature of the changes such as adjustments in patterns of daily living, sexual activity, roles and responsibilities and socializing. Review normal patterns and consider how these can be maintained within the limitations of the disease. Help spouse to reassign priorities with patient care as the focus, and devise ways in which patients can be included in the usual activities.

- Acknowledge that when spouses make adjustments in usual patterns, this forms part of the work of caring and its value should not be underestimated. Affirm spouses for their efforts.
- Reinforce the need for spouses to care for themselves for the sake of their own health.

Children

- Examine how existing communication patterns with the patient, the well parent, their siblings, and their own spouse and children exacerbate or relieve the distress.
- Review the effects of the changes on their own spouses and children and the degree that they might be able to help. If spouses and children from the family of procreation can be more independent, this allows more time to be available for the ill parent.
- Assess the developmental needs of their children in understanding illness and death. Provide information about children's reactions to dying and death so parents may avert negative behavior from fear and lack of attention.
- Acknowledge that when adult children make changes in their usual roles and responsibilities, this forms part of the work of caring and should be recognized as such.
- Examine how siblings may share responsibilities for the care of the ill parent so as to distribute the work.
- Hold a family conference as one way of planning how to divide the responsibilities.
- Encourage children to include some social activities for themselves as a means of time out. This replenishes their energy and enables them to continue with the extra demands over time.

CHAPTER 6

Searching for Meaning

*When all this happened to me . . . I didn't know who I was
. . . Now I'm confident, I know who I am, I know what I'm
thinking. It's been a struggle, growing up, and here I am
sixty-two and I feel like I'm finally growing up. This is
obviously leading to something valuable.*

Mrs. L., age sixty-two, ovarian cancer

During this component, family members examine and seek answers that help them to understand and come to terms with their situation. The focus of searching for meaning varies for patients, spouses, and children. Patients take a journey into themselves, reflecting more on the spiritual aspects of life. Spouses concentrate on the meaning of their relationship with the patient and how the illness has in some ways contributed to their personal growth. Children reflect on the implications of the experience on all aspects of their lives. However, not all individuals searched for meaning.

PATIENTS

Patients try to put their experience in context and endure the turmoil. They try to make sense of the situation by connecting with their inner and spiritual selves, connecting with others or with nature. Connecting with self involves a re-examination and affirmation of values and a possible change in priorities. As one man said, "The spiritual thing has always been at the back of my mind, but it's developed more . . . When you're sick like that, your attitude changes towards life. You come not to be afraid of death . . ."

Deepening connections with others helps patients in their search for meaning. One woman described the satisfaction from her last year of teaching: "I had been able to get this group of students to cooperate with my problems to a remarkable degree . . . so it was the

best year for bonding with students that I ever had." This same
woman perceived another positive outcome in closer relationships
with her stepsons which she attributed to their concern for her
during her illness. Joining groups where similar concerns can be
shared—a Bible study group or a self-help group, for instance—
helps some patients.

A connection with nature minimizes feelings of loss. Patients
focus on what is alive and growing. One woman described a driving
trip to the country where she derived

> a lot of pleasure from seeing a porcupine on the road, seeing
> cattle being taken to the open range, seeing calypso orchids in
> their prime . . . things like that are very helpful to me to mini-
> mize the feelings of that loss.

Another patient found meaning in sitting and "watching crea-
tion."

In a common strategy, patients reflect on their lives or some
significant aspect: "Not many people have enjoyed their years after
they have quit work like I have, and I really appreciate them more
than ever now . . . I realize what a good life I've had." Another
patient reflected on his ability to always work: "I had perfect
health up to the day of age sixty-nine. I was never sick. I worked
hard."

Patients pay attention to the ordinary aspects of life.

> I've had time to focus on things . . . like my appetite which for
> seventy years I took for granted. . . . You are more acutely aware
> of the things immediately around you like the amazing number
> of flowers and plants I have received . . . and the number of
> cards I have had from people.

The ill person may appreciate the experience of other sick people,
and gain some solace from knowing that he or she is not
alone: ". . . I'm sharing some of this sickness that other people have
had. I'm not happy about it, but now that I have it, I know what
those other people went through."

In a final strategy, patients do good, or nurture others:

> If I could just help somebody, I would. I would feel better about
> it. It doesn't have to be my family . . . because of the help that
> I've received, I've got to try and return some of it somehow . . . I
> want to help people and I think that's helping me.

Many patients participated in the research study which served as the basis for this book because of their wish to help others.

When patients search for meaning, this engenders satisfaction and a sense of usefulness instead of despair and hopelessness. It enhances the quality of patients' lives. In the words of one patient: "Having some gains in a season of losses."

SPOUSES

Spouses often focus on relationships, on the positive in the situation and on personal growth. They appreciate and enjoy family members more, spend more time together, and in case of disharmony, tolerate one another. These strategies renew their sense of the value of human attachments. They see the positive and identify the good that comes from the experience. To some degree, this helps balance an overwhelmingly negative situation. One man described how the situation contributed to the growth of his relationship with his wife. He focused on the positive aspect, saying,

> Why do we have this, why are we blessed with this? I have no idea. It's a shame. But I think we can cope with it because we don't look at the severing of the relationship, we look at it as a beautiful time in our lives.

Spouses realize these positive aspects might not have occurred without the cancer experience. As one woman said, "We were very close, but it's drawn us closer. There are a lot of things that the cancer has helped. Maybe we would have just gone on our own way and not paid attention to those things." She referred to the gains as: "his family—his brothers and sisters were drawn very much closer . . . and our daughter re-evaluated (what) she thought was important and realized . . . menial things are not worth fretting and stewing over."

In another aspect of searching for meaning, spouses often reflect on their new level of spiritual awareness. Some grow spiritually as they explore their faith although this opens painful or difficult areas. Some pray, read religious materials, see spiritual resource people and talk with friends. The experience does not devastate them. "It would certainly be just a big black spot in our lives at this time, but we know that is not the case." Their strong spiritual belief supports them through their search for meaning: "It's like that light shining through the kitchen window. If we didn't have that light to grab on to, and know that we have something beyond, I think that it would just be impossible to live with." These spouses experience a painful, but acceptable, challenge to their belief systems. They acknowledge the pain, and reflect on how they grow from the experience.

However, when spouses use their belief systems dogmatically they feel an overwhelming pressure, anguish and despair: "Black is black and white is white," one spouse said to communicate his belief about the events he faced, which left no room for expressions of uncertainty or fear. Either they already have the answer: "God has let these things happen to us for a trial or whatever, and we have to accept it"; or, they find the answer in their religious beliefs. They maintain a rigid stance; there is little room for questions, and as a result, little search for meaning.

Also, not every spouse searches for meaning to the same degree. If spouses concentrate on why the cancer diagnosis has occurred in the first place, or if they focus on the negative aspects of managing the illness, they do not discuss issues related to searching for meaning. They focus more on "enduring" the experience than on "growing" through it. In the words of one spouse, ". . . it's a test of endurance . . ." They feel they have done the best they can as do the other spouses, but they do not feel any satisfaction from the experience. They wait for it to end.

CHILDREN

Children come face-to-face with mortality, with their own vulnerability and with the impact on their future. Their search for meaning evolves from this. They identify one major strategy: the re-evaluation of their attitudes, beliefs and values in relation to themselves, their family of origin, their family of procreation, and their lifestyle. Some resolve to make significant changes.

Adult children reflect on their lives and ask questions about their priorities and goals. The terminal experience influences the major decisions they face at this point in their lives, in relationships, families, careers, health, and lifestyle. "It puts in perspective how important some of our goals are . . . having our mortgage paid off . . . having financial independence and being able to retire at a decent age . . . it made us reevaluate our values . . ."

Children may implement better self care or change their perspective on materialism. They express concern for their own children—those they dream of who will not know their grandparent, or those they already have. They want their children to learn from the experience in a positive way: "... the oldest one is now at Mom's house five or six times a week, and I think he's learned to appreciate her a lot more."

Adult children do not focus on positive aspects of the terminal experience as much as do spouses and patients. In the words of one son, "The only good to come out of this experience, is for it not to have happened." Also some children focus on the regrets of the past and how they could possibly be ameliorated. One daughter recreated the relationship she wished she had with her mother. She spent time hugging her mother and said, "I feel. . . I finally found the mother I never had." She did not focus on how the experience affected her present life and her own children, nor on how the experience might affect her future life.

When the search for meaning focuses primarily on the past, children put everything else on hold, including the well being of their own children. Adult children spend time replacing what they believe was neglected. After an unsuccessful attempt to reconcile with her mother, one daughter said she wanted to say, "Please don't go and leave me like this, I don't want the last (meeting) to be (on) a bad note." Then, one day when things were better, she thought, "O.K., if you've got to go, go on a day like this, don't do it when you've just snapped at me and hurt me so much that I walk out and then I get a call and it's over." In her words, the dilemma "ripped her apart all the time" and she had very little energy left for her son.

GUIDELINES FOR CARE

Practitioners help families search for meaning by enabling them to tell their personal story and make sense of it. It is vitally important for practitioners to appreciate that when families talk about their current situation and their recollections of past illness and losses, this is not simply idle conversation. It is part of the process of making sense of the situation and coping with feelings. It is also important for practitioners to realize that much of the search for meaning involves examination of relationships within the family.

Patients

- Appreciate that searching for meaning involves patients' re-examining themselves, their relatedness to others, and their spiritual beliefs.

- Encourage life reviews and reminiscing.
- Provide opportunities for patients to share their introspections with you or make them aware of volunteer or other support groups with whom they can share their thoughts and concerns.
- Focus on the positive; reinforce activities they can still accomplish or participate in.
- Examine how patients may help or nurture others as a means of reciprocating the care and support they receive, even if this involves sharing their experiences or knowledge with others as opposed to helping them physically.

Spouses

- Discuss how the experience of serious illness can be painful and difficult, but may also be a time when positives emerge, such as enhanced family relationships.
- Provide opportunities for spouses to talk about the changes in their lives and the belief systems they associate or attribute to those changes.
- Provide opportunities for spouses to consider those aspects of themselves or their relationships which changed in a positive direction because of their experience.

Children

- Explain that the experience of illness often forces people to a far-reaching examination of their values, beliefs, and goals. This exploration may extend to themselves, their family of origin, family of procreation and their lifestyle.
- Suggest approaches for personal reflection such as journal writing.
- Suggest approaches to facilitate interactions between family members such as writing letters or exchanging tapes.

CHAPTER 7

Living Day-To-Day

*Live one day to the next. That's the only thing that's work-
ing. Worry about tomorrow, tomorrow. You live for today,
today.*

P., son, father has lung cancer

Two reasons account for a briefer description of this component
of the transition versus others. First, not all people with a terminal illness reach this point, and therefore fewer data exist.
Second—and more important—although this component of the transition addresses painful, difficult tasks, it does not entail the same
agonizing, soul-searching struggle.

The search for meaning appears to form a bridge between
the struggle thus far and a new perspective. When people have
found some meaning and can put the situation into perspective, they
experience less turmoil. They see more clearly the need to live
day-to-day and make the most of the time they have left. For
children, living day-to-day creates its own stressors.

PATIENTS

When patients live day-to-day they "make the most of it" and
"focus on the present." They plan only for the short-term and accept
events the way they are rather than worry about the future. One
man said, "But, that's the situation as it is. So, I don't get down
about it and (become) pessimistic about it. I think every day is a day,
and sometimes I can do more and sometimes less." And another:
"There's not much point in going over things in the past: not much
point in projecting yourself too far into the future either. It's the
current time that counts." Patients maintain a positive attitude and
keep life as normal as possible and as a result become more content
and appreciate what life still has to offer. Sometimes, despite severe

pain, patients think "every day is still quite precious." They focus on life and living: "I think I really appreciate the 'now' more than anything else. Each day I thank God for waking up in the morning and thank Him at the end of the day."

Not all patients focus on living-day-to-day to the same degree. For example, even though his was one of the longest interviews, one man talked very little about living day to day. His statements about making the best of it were qualified or minimized; he focused on "getting through" the illness: "I'm not going to talk about any of those woes or sickness . . . I have no intention of talking like that. I'm just going to . . . if I get worse and worse, I'll just go through it."

SPOUSES

Spouses know the near future will not include their ill partners and they live for today. They spend as much quality time together as possible: "I want to be able to live my life with D. as long as we can. There are some things that we can't do, but there are other ways that we can make the best of it."

The spouse makes more effort to get along with the patient which results in greater satisfaction and enjoyment: ". . . I'm spending as much time with him as I can and enjoying every minute of it, so maybe we're not off in Hawaii or something, but we're in our backyard and enjoying being together."

However, not all spouses can appreciate the intrinsic value of living-day-to-day. Rather than enjoy, they endure. One spouse reflected on her life of hardship and remarked that it continued in the same way: "I've always had a hard life, and it hasn't changed." If the partners find difficulty in each other's company, they tend to avoid one another so conflicts do not arise. Nearly every day becomes a trial which they endure.

CHILDREN

Living day-to-day places great demands on adult children who care for the patient and manage their own lives simultaneously. They do not have the luxury of deferring obligations the way spouses can. In fact, one child who did this, did not cope well. Her behavior interfered with the patient-spousal relationship and the functioning of her family of origin and family of procreation.

Children try to avoid a constant state of worry so they can continue with their daily lives. "Live one day to the next. That's the only thing that's working. Worry about tomorrow, tomorrow. You live for today." This means they do what they can for the patient and move on with their own lives. They realize their parents do not want them to put their lives on hold and they try not to neglect the important aspects. One daughter visited her mother regularly and knew her mother supported her work-related travel plans: "It's not fair to my mother either for me to put everything on hold until she dies . . . I have an opportunity to go to Montreal and I'm going to go. If anything happens, we'll deal with that then." In this way, the adult children meet their obligations as best they can although they incur costs in terms of physical and psychological energy.

GUIDELINES FOR CARE

In this component, families make subtle shifts in their orientation to living with a dying member. They move from thinking there is no future, to making the most of the time still available. Sensitive practitioners listen extremely carefully for the subtle shifts and gauge a family's readiness for a new orientation. It is a time when discussions do not focus entirely on the illness and its consequences, but on life and living.

Patients

- Ensure effective control of symptoms so that the patient makes the most of the time available. Assess the need for aids for independent living (for instance, walkers, raised toilet seats).
- Encourage patients to make short-term plans to participate in those activities or visits with family and friends that bring the most enjoyment.
- Without minimizing their losses and concerns about the future, affirm their ability to appreciate and make the most of the time they have left.

Spouses

- Review resources such as home support services, volunteers, or nursing services that relieve spouses of some duties so that they spend the desired time with the patient.

- Affirm spouses for their ability to make the most of the time available.

Children

- Discuss the need for a balance between helping their parents and carrying on with their own activities. Acknowledge this can be one of the most difficult aspects of caring for a sick parent, both physically and psychologically.
- Assist the children to consider how they (and the grandchildren) can arrange to spend as much time as possible with the patient and to feel comfortable with the decisions they make.

CHAPTER 8

Preparing for Death

We've made all the arrangements just in case something does happen to Dad. Dad never had a will. We never spoke about that kind of financial stuff. So, we got a will drafted and he signed it and I went through all his personal papers to see what he had.

E., son, father has cancer of the bladder

In preparing for death, patients, spouses, and children come to terms with the practical aspects of dying. They make plans individually and together. Preparing for death refers not only to practical aspects but also to the more complex domains of cognitive and emotional preparation.

PATIENTS

Practical preparations for death include legal aspects:

I've made all my arrangements. I know that I'm not going to be living much longer, and if we know that, then why not accept it? I have talked it over with my wife, and made sure that everything is in order.

Patients often focus on the care of their family members. One man encouraged his wife to learn to drive the car: ". . . she has given in and started to drive again which I am glad to see because then if anything happens to me, it would be better for her to have transportation . . ." A mother, concerned about her daughter's well-being after the death, told her daughter about a bereavement group. Patients also attend to seemingly mundane details such as house repairs.

Patients have their family's needs uppermost in preparing for the actual event of death. Some express concern about the location of death, and about what happens at the time of death. They want the event to go smoothly for the family. One woman prepared her family: "They know who to report to and who to get in touch with in case anything goes wrong."

Many patients focus on the practical arrangements after death. One woman told her daughter,

> Get me cremated. Get an urn for my ashes and put me in with your Dad's grave. Don't bother with the coffin . . . I don't approve of spending huge amounts of money on expensive caskets and then having them cremated.

For some patients, preparing for death involves reminiscing about their lives and those events which had given them happiness or a sense of accomplishment. They look through photo albums of enjoyable holidays, recall good times with family and friends and remember personal moments of enjoyment throughout their lives. These patients recognize the importance of creating situations which leave family members with happy memories. One patient accompanied her family to church on Father's Day despite her discomfort, as she realized this would be the last time. She also left tangible memories in the afghans she made. Another patient and his wife planned and went on their last holiday together.

When patients use specific strategies for preparing for death, communicate openly about their wishes and attend to the details surrounding the death and afterwards, they have a sense of completion and satisfaction. They have done the best they can to make it as easy as possible for family members. Patients generally believe they "had a good life," even those who report many difficulties.

SPOUSES

Spouses complete their preparations in partnership with the patients and center on meeting the patient's wishes, even when this is difficult: "I don't know that I like the thought of him dying at home, because it's going to be like a knife . . . but if that's what he wants, how can I deny it? It's his home too." Another spouse said, "He doesn't want a ritual service . . . I guess what you could do is have a memorial service and have a couple of friends say something nice about him. I hope we can handle it all right."

As part of preparing for death spouses allude to the future without the patient. Some spouses do this to a greater degree than others. All that one woman said was, "It's ... hard to talk about death ... and hard to get along without him. That's a very traumatic thing. I have never been alone." Another woman repeatedly discussed proposed changes to the house as a method of preparing herself.

Spouses often attend to practical details while the patient is still relatively well. They make plans and this affords them some comfort. When the spouse and patient differ in their wishes, the spouse often makes a determined effort at support: "If she said, 'I want to spend my last hours here in this house,' that would be her decision. If she said that she wanted to go to palliative care, that would be her decision." Despite their commitment to the patient's request, some spouses wonder whether they can carry through. They hope they will manage or that someone will stay with them.

Some spouses believe they will be spiritually reunited after their own death, which makes the anticipation of their future without the patient easier.

CHILDREN

Adult children have a wider circle of people involved in preparations for death than spouses, especially those children with families of their own. They assist their parents with legal arrangements and spend time with the ill parent as a strategy for preparing for death: "I try to be there and try to make that person's last bit of life bearable, and happier than it could be if he were alone." They frequently agonize over how much they should discuss death and its implications with the ill parent, but when they do so, the discussion reassures the parent.

Children also reassure the parent that those left behind will be cared for. One son-in-law, the husband of B., told the patient he had often wondered what it would be like to be in his position. The patient said, "I feel I have a better place prepared, but I am worried about leaving Mom." The son-in-law assured him that he and B. would always be there for her. At this, B. said, "... Dad looked so peaceful ... he smiled and nodded, and there was no need to say anything else."

Adult children often keep their own children informed and take them to visit the grandparent, which facilitates their own more-frequent visits. They prepare the children for the grandparent's death:

> I've explained to my son that Grand-dad is probably dying, and
> he has accepted that so he wants to see my Dad as much as he
> can. He's just about five . . . and he just sits and colors pictures
> for him and they talk.

Adult children spend time with siblings and help prepare them
for the death. One son talked of his sister's pain when she realized
how ill her father was:

> She was in tears most of the way home. She is a much more
> emotional person than I, but I think she had seen something
> that she hadn't seen before . . . it shook her, she thought the
> time was very near that Dad would pass away.

The adult children most closely involved in the situation feel an
acute sense of responsibility to inform and help others make
decisions about when to visit. They initiate the interactions, but
frequently feel frustrated:

> We were all together for a week, and everyone found different
> things to talk about. Nobody ever wanted to do it (talk about the
> gravity of the situation). And, finally I said, "We have to sit down
> and talk. There's never going to be a really good time. We must
> talk about what Dad wants . . . death at home, supportive care,
> aggressive measures."

Adult children anticipate the actual time of death and the
funeral, the well parent's future without their spouse and their own
future without the parent, as another way of preparing for death.
One daughter said, "It's hard knowing that you're going to have to
deal with that (the death), but it's also nice knowing that there's a
place like the cancer hospital and the people in there." Another
daughter said, ". . . I'm trying to build myself up emotionally . . . to
be able to handle that (the funeral) when it does happen . . . you
don't want to see the end, but you're getting ready, . . . all the time,
every day, you're getting ready."

One son expressed deep concern for the future of the well parent:
". . . It's already very hard for her, and it's going to be worse."
Children also worry about their own future without their parent: "I
find myself sometimes thinking ahead to what it's going to be like,
and I just can't. I don't know what it's going to be like."

However, when adult children give themselves permission to
think about the past, the present and the future, despite the bittersweet nature of remembrances, this helps them anticipate the

future without the ill parent and they appreciate the relationship they had:

> I'm very thankful that I've had all the years with my mother. Maybe that helped me through it . . . even if she had died this past month, I still have a lot of memories of her that I have been very thankful for.

The various strategies children use induce a sense of satisfaction with the plans developed and decisions made.

GUIDELINES FOR CARE

In helping families prepare for death, practitioners must be comfortable talking about the inevitability of death, describing the dying process, and helping families make plans for wills and funerals. Practitioners do not force or push, but also do not turn away because of their own insecurities about dying and death.

Patients

- Discuss patients' wishes about the circumstances of their death (place of care, people in attendance, funeral preferences). Encourage them to discuss these with their family. Acknowledge these discussions may be difficult for them and their family. Affirm them for their courage to face a difficult issue.
- Encourage patients to attend to practical details such as making a will and distributing possessions.
- Explain that when patients reminisce with family and friends they celebrate the happy times and accomplishments of their lives.
- Encourage patients to do important "last things," such as a special holiday or completion of a project as a legacy for their family.

Spouses

- Encourage spouses to make plans for the funeral while the patient can make his or her wishes known. Although difficult, this process ensures patients share their concerns.
- Provide information about the dying process. If the plan is for death at home, provide information about management (such as

pronouncement of death) and resources available to help. Discuss who will be present to support them at the time of death.

- Provide opportunities for spouses to express their concerns about the future without their spouse.
- Provide opportunities for spouses to reminisce about the relationship with the patient and their life together. This acts as a way to say "good-bye."

Children

- Acknowledge that when children spend time with the patient this forms part of caring even if they feel as though they do not do anything.
- Explain that when children talk with the ill parent about death, they offer reassurance that his or her wishes will be taken into account and that he or she will not be abandoned.
- Encourage children to bring the family together to talk about and plan the management of the impending death. Affirm them for taking the initiative to deal with a difficult and painful subject.
- Provide adult children with information about their own children's developmental understanding of death. Explain the importance of age-appropriate information and of visits to their sick grandparent.
- Provide opportunities for adult children to reminisce about the past with their parent. Acknowledge such remembrances will have a bittersweet quality associated with them.

DISCUSSION

The transition of fading away that we have presented affirms our initial deliberations concerning how to approach the investigation of terminal cancer from a family perspective. Had we selected one or more of the variables we identified as potentially significant to the family's experience, we would, no doubt, have learned a great deal about those particular concepts. Indeed, other investigators have attempted to understand the situation of dying for the family unit through studies of coping strategies, stress management, anticipatory grief, and systems theory to name a few. Their findings add to the body of knowledge about how to help families ease the pain and grief associated with impending death. However, such findings provide limited insight into the totality of an exceptionally complex experience. This approach reminds us of the Hindu fable "The Blind Men and the Elephant" [1]. This fable tells of six blind men who attempt to describe an elephant. The first happened to fall against the elephant's side and decided the elephant is like a wall. The second felt the tusk and said the elephant is like a spear, round and smooth and sharp. The third touched the squirming trunk and decided the elephant is much like a snake. The fourth felt the knee and said the elephant is like a tree. The fifth took hold of the ear and declared the elephant is like a fan. The last man seized the swinging tail and said the elephant is most like a rope. According to the fable, they argued loud and long and each kept strongly to his own opinion. Though each was somewhat right about the part he touched, all were wrong about the whole elephant. Like the people in the fable, researchers have identified different parts of the experience of dying. This occurs because they ask different questions and approach those questions from different belief systems or models which describe human behavior. In this manner, they identify different parts of the same whole. Our efforts focused on describing the whole. In so doing, we, too, identified a number of concepts relevant to the family's experience, but no one concept in and of itself sufficiently described the process. Only when taken together, did they describe the entirety of the family's experience—the transition of fading away.

When families have a member who has terminal cancer, they experience the transition of fading away. This transition incorporates several components that are interrelated and intertwined. The transition must begin with the patient's redefinition of self, and other family members' redefinition of the patient. Redefining continues throughout the experience, but once the family begins this process, other components also come into play. The patient confronts the possibility of being a burden and family members grapple with being burdened by the extra responsibilities inherent in caring for a dying member. The family struggles with several paradoxes which derive from the central paradox of the patient living with cancer while dying from cancer. Every one of the family faces major changes in their lives and searches for meaning to find some way of coming to terms with the experience. As the end draws near, the patient and other family members live day to day and prepare for the impending death. A word of caution is in order here. Using the components to "label" points in time would be a misinterpretation of our findings. For example, to describe Mr. Jones as "living day to day," implying that he has "passed through" the other components and has now reached the end of the transition negates the fact that components overlap with one another and are not sequential.

Redefining is an essential first step to the process of fading away. It is crucial, however, to point out that the components as we have described them do not occur in sequence. Though distinctly described, the components are interrelated. They can be likened to the threads of a tapestry in the making. Threads of varying colors and textures are interwoven to create the evolving scene. Unlike a tapestry which is eventually complete as a work of art, the portraits of families facing the transition of fading away are always in process.

We found that the family cannot be understood as separate from its members. Each family member experiences the transition in his or her own unique way. However, because they interact with one another, they influence each other, and how they, as a unit, experience the transition. We concur with Friedman who defines the family as a human social system with distinct characteristics that is composed of individuals whose characteristics are equally distinct [2, p. 211]. It is this which makes working with families in palliative care so complex and challenging. To provide optimal palliative care, health care professionals must take into account both individual factors and family systems factors, such as interactions among family members. To focus only on the individual members or on the family unit conjures up the image portrayed by the Hindu fable. The picture would be incomplete. In the preceding chapters, we described guidelines for working with individual members as they deal with the various components of the transition. In the next chapter, we provide additional guidelines for working with families in palliative care when the children in the family are teenagers. In the subsequent chapter, we turn our attention to the family as a unit and how its functioning affects how the transition of fading away is experienced.

> *It's a sad ending, you know, it's a sad time, but it . . .*
> *maybe it's a new beginning to something.*
> Mr. X.'s son, father has prostate cancer

The thoughts of this family member capture the essence of the transition of fading away. The life of the patient and the family as they have known it is ending. The ending brings with it imposed changes, sadness, burdens, turmoil, and pain. But, paradoxically and tentatively, a new beginning emerges that accepts death and embraces life and living.

REFERENCES

1. Six Blind Men and an Elephant, in *Clever Stories of Many Nations*, J. E. Saxe (ed.), Ticknor and Fields, Boston, Massachusettes, pp. 59-64, 1865.
2. M. L. Friedman, The Concept of Family Nursing, *Journal of Advanced Nursing, 14*, pp. 211-216, 1989.

CHAPTER 9

When the Children are Teenagers

This chapter elaborates on the transition of fading away from the perspective of teenagers whose parents were terminally ill. The research from which this chapter was derived was not part of the original research project, but was conducted by a graduate student, Janie Brown, RN, MSN, MA, as part of her thesis, using the same research approach as in the larger studies.

> *I don't like it. I feel kind of trapped. Like why is this happening to me? You can't leave it. You always know you have to come home to it.*
> fifteen-year-old daughter of man dying of lung cancer

The previous chapters in this book include descriptions of the experience of families who are caring for one member with end-stage cancer as a process of fading-away; a series of components describing the transition from living with cancer to dying from cancer. These chapters described the experience of patients, spouses, and adult children living with terminal cancer in the family. All of the adult children were over the age of eighteen years and hence none of the families studied included the experience of teenagers. What is the experience of younger children, specifically teenagers who are younger than eighteen? To answer such a question is to validate and expand the description of the transition of fading away.

The following chapter describes the experience of eleven teenagers who were living with a parent in the advanced stages of cancer, within the context of the transition of fading away.

TEENAGE DEVELOPMENT

Teenagers often present challenges even to the well family. In order to master the developmental task of emotional and physical separation from parents, they withdraw emotionally from the family unit and intensify relationships outside of it [1]. When their parent is ill, teenagers are pulled in the opposite direction from this natural developmental course into re-intensified contact with parents [2]. They often feel that their freedom has been restricted which can lead to feelings of isolation from their friends [3]. They may demonstrate acting-out behavior, extreme anxiety or poor scholastic achievements [2, 4].

The feelings and behavior changes experienced by teenagers living with an ill parent undoubtedly have ramifications on the functioning of the family as a whole as it struggles to live day-to-day with the impending loss of a family member.

FADING AWAY

Families who are living with one member who is terminally ill describe that, at a certain point in time, they come to the sudden realization that death is inevitable. This realization is triggered by a change in the patient's physical condition such as increased weakness, decreased mobility, or diminishing mental abilities. Although the realization is sudden, fading away is considered by patients and family members to be a process which occurs over time, as the patient's condition slowly deteriorates.

Although teenagers acknowledge that their parent is likely to die, they view their parent's physical condition as a series of illness events, which make up the process of slow decline. Each time the parent's physical condition worsens it triggers the realization in the teenager that their parent is going to die: "The only time I am deathly afraid he will die is when I see him bunched up over the toilet or deathly pale and lost twenty-five pounds and not eating anything, when he is physically sick."

There is often extreme distress for teenagers each time their parent's physical condition declines: "I was terrified when he threw up that he was going to die right then and there. I didn't want to be there. I couldn't help. I just ran out of the room." Teenagers find it difficult, therefore, to predict how close to death their parent is at any given time and become extremely fearful each time their parent's physical condition visibly worsens.

Teenagers have little understanding of the expected course of the dying process which is comprised of periods of decline alternating with periods of stability. When their parent's condition stabilizes, teenagers do not perceive this stable period as part of the overall decline but as a time to be hopeful that their parent will recover. The more physically well their parent appears to be during the stable periods, the less afraid teenagers are that their parent will die: "I was worried when he was in the hospital. Compared to that he is better, so I don't think anything is wrong."

GUIDELINES FOR CARE

Practitioners working with teenagers can help them understand that the dying process usually includes periods of decline and periods of relative stability. This understanding may reduce the severity of distress teenagers feel each time their parent displays worsening physical symptoms. It may also help them more accurately assess how close death actually is at any given time.

- Assess the teenager's level of knowledge about the physical condition of their parent and their willingness to learn more about their parent's situation.
- If there is an expressed willingness to learn more, explain the dying process in language that is understandable to the teenager.
- Assist him or her to understand the likely course of events and the meaning of each new physical symptom in terms of significance to their parent's overall condition.
- If the teenager does not wish to learn more, accept that he or she has chosen to shield themselves from the reality that their parent is going to die. Shielding enables the teenagers to pursue the normal tasks of adolescence and to get on with their own lives.
- Observe the teenager for signs of distress and provide opportunities for the teenager to ask questions about their parent's condition and symptoms, and for them to express their feelings about the situation.

REDEFINING

Redefining requires a shift in how individuals view themselves and others in order to successfully adjust to the reality that death is inevitable. Redefining occurs as the patient and family members accommodate to changes in the patient's health status and begin to let go of the old view of the patient, seeing him or her in a different way. This readjustment helps both the patient and the family to cope with the losses and to identify any gains they have acquired, or anticipate acquiring, in the future.

Teenagers demonstrate a reluctance to redefine their parent, despite obvious deterioration in their parent's physical condition. They hold on to the old view of their parent as much as they can by trying not to think about the fact that their parent is seriously ill: "When I look at him I don't see that he has cancer really. I just see him normally like I always see him. That's the whole point, I never think about it. I try not to think about it."

This strategy of not thinking about it helps teenagers to quell their fears about living in the future without their parent:

> I'm basically just living my life normally and doing everything the same as I would otherwise. I don't want to think ahead about what it could be. If he died then I guess I'd really understand what it's like to be alone, like having to do all this stuff myself and not having them to be always there for me. That always screws me up when I think about that.

By maintaining the old view of their parents and not redefining them, teenagers do not need to redefine themselves as living in the future without their parents and hence need not face their fears of abandonment.

Teenagers' hesitation in redefining their parents is most apparent during periods of stability when their parents have fewer obvious physical symptoms. At these times, teenagers often feel that their parents could do more for themselves and that they are using their illness to take advantage of the teenagers' willingness to help: "Sometimes I don't know if he really is tired or whether he is taking advantage of the situation, so I get mad sometimes. Like he walks all over me because he knows I feel sorry for him."

Redefining requires an adjustment to the fact that the ill person is vulnerable to death. Teenagers do not redefine themselves as being vulnerable to death as a consequence of realizing that their parent is going to die. In fact, their behavior indicates that they believe they are invincible. Many teenagers describe risk-taking or self-destructive behaviors such as smoking, taking drugs, overeating and engaging in unprotected sexual intercourse: "Well what could be worse than my Dad dying. I don't really care if I am pregnant. One life ends and another begins. I'd be doing it for my Dad." The teenagers did not question their own mortality, but challenged it by engaging in self-destructive, as opposed to self-caring behaviors.

GUIDELINES FOR CARE

Practitioners can best understand teenagers' reluctance to redefine their parents from a developmental framework. Thinking that their parent is going to die demands that teenagers face the reality that they must be independent and fully emotionally separated from their parents. Most teenagers face the process of individuation/separation with great ambivalence [5]. They vacillate between the desire for independence and the security afforded by childhood [5]. The security of parents and home is a necessary prerequisite to healthy separation from parents and, hence, any threat to that security is liable to create difficulty in separation for the teenager. Having a parent who is seriously ill disrupts the normal process of breaking away for teenagers, as their security is shattered and they feel pulled back into the family.

- Acknowledge that the situation represents a threat to the teenager's security and anticipate questions related to security issues for their future.

- Suggest that parents provide as much reassurance as possible to the teenagers about what will happen at home if, in fact, the parent does die, e.g., will the rest of the family stay living in the family home, who will take over the roles and responsibilities of the ill parent, etc.?

- Assess risk-taking behaviors of the teenager such as drug and alcohol consumption, eating disorders, sexual practices and acting-out behaviors. Assist the teenager to understand the risks to their own health and help them to identify other less harmful ways of coping with their situation.

BURDENING

When patients become unable to take care of their own personal needs or to fulfill former roles and responsibilities, they rely on family members to become involved. The patient often feels that this is burdensome for the family. Family members, while they often feel exhausted, also feel satisfied with their contribution. Teenagers feel significantly burdened by living with a terminally-ill parent, especially because it may require spending more time at home, taking on more responsibilities, and repressing feelings.

Teenagers often spend much more time at home than they did before their parent became ill. Many think that they should spend even more time with family than they already are. They often feel trapped, particularly those who are expected to provide care to the ill parent. Older teenagers also feel unable to seriously consider moving out of the family home to live independently.

They often resent the increase in household chores that is expected of them when one parent is ill because it interferes with their own activities: "The housework and grocery shopping. We all have to do quite a bit more. I find it frustrating because this is my summer."

Although the increase in household chores often leads to serious arguments between siblings, teenagers also describe the burden of having to keep the peace at home: "You have to be careful what you say, because if you say something wrong, she's going to explode. Before it was easier, you could just say whatever or do whatever. Now you just kind of watch what you say."

Teenagers often try to keep a lid on their feelings: "I don't ever let it surface as anger. I don't want to cause any more ripples. I don't want to cause any more problems. There are already enough. I just want to keep everything as calm as possible." They rarely talk about their feelings with family members or friends because "I don't like getting the feelings out. I think I'm scared of my emotions." They feel that their friends cannot really understand what it is like to be living with a parent who is very ill and so they choose not to share their feelings. Repressing feelings and not talking about their fears and concerns is a major burden for teenagers.

Burdening, then, is a major phenomenon for teenagers. They feel the burden of having to stay at home more and of having to take on more of the household chores which often leads to animosity between siblings. They also feel restricted when considering a move away from home to live independently, because of feelings of obligation to be there for the ill parent. They feel the burden of having to keep the peace at home by watching what they do and what they say, for fear of upsetting their parent. They repress their feelings which precipitates emotional outbursts and arguments, and they find it very difficult to communicate their fears to anyone. Teenagers' burdens focus on the conflict between what they want to do and what they feel they should do: their sense of duty or obligation to be at home more and their desire to meet their own needs for independence.

GUIDELINES FOR CARE

Normal growth and development for teenagers expects a natural movement toward independence, a gradual physical and emotional separation from parents. Much of the burden experienced by teenagers is a reflection of this normal development. A sensitive practitioner will appreciate the necessity for teenagers to continue to pursue their developmental path despite the difficult family situation at home.

- Assist parents to understand the teenagers' resentment at having to stay home more and at having to take on added responsibilities within the context of normal growth and development. Provide information on available resources for home support services to minimize these added responsibilities, particularly with regard to providing physical care for their ill parent.
- Encourage parents to allow their teenagers to carry on with their usual activities outside the home.
- Provide opportunities for teenagers to talk about their feelings in order to minimize emotional outbursts and repression of feelings.

STRUGGLING WITH PARADOX

Teenagers face many paradoxes as they struggle with the developmental need to move away from family to independence, while also feeling the compulsion to stay at home and be there for their ill parent. Teenagers do not express the need to spend as much time as possible with their parent before they die. They lack the same ability to look into the future and see the inevitability of death. Hence, they do not feel the need to make the most of the time left with their parents.

The paradoxes teenagers face center on: wanting their parent to live while wishing it were over; pushing thoughts of death away while dwelling on death; caring about and resenting their parent; longing to be closer and not knowing how to be closer; and having questions to ask but not wanting to know the answers.

Like adult children, teenagers struggle with the paradox of wanting their parents to live and wishing the cancer would go away, as well as wishing it would all be over. Unlike some adult children who wish it would be over to relieve their parent's suffering, teenagers wish it would be over to relieve their own suffering:

> Sometimes I wish he would get better and sometimes I wish he wouldn't get better. I know it's mean to say but that's just the way I feel. I don't want to feel like this forever. I just want it to be over. I just want some normalcy again, some stability in my life.

Teenagers are concerned with the disruption to their lives which prevents them from getting on with establishing their own identity and independence from family.

Teenagers have a tendency to try and push away the reality that their parent is going to die. Many talk of trying not to think about it and yet at the same time they also dwell on the fact that their parent may die:

> No, nothing much has changed actually. It's just like it hasn't hit me in an overall way. I just don't think about it really. . . . You just start thinking, it makes you think about what things would be like, what you would do, what would happen to the family?

Teenagers experience the paradox of feeling empathy for their sick parent and wanting to do things for them, while also feeling resentful toward them for taking advantage of the teenager's willingness to help:

> It's kind of brought us together because something has happened and you feel more for her, like not pity but you want to help her. But sometimes I don't like it because she uses it more as a weapon. That bothers me.

Older teenagers often acknowledge an increasing level of closeness between themselves and their parent. Younger teenagers, however, express ambivalence regarding a longing to draw closer to their ill parent and not knowing how to do this:

> I want to talk to him more but it's not something that's going to come easy to me, the wanting is there logically, but emotionally it isn't. I want to share more with him but it's so hard and I couldn't care less really. I have a strong sense that I don't want to, but I do want to because I do love him and I don't want him to die thinking that maybe I don't love him.

Many teenagers feel that they have all the information they wish about their parent's disease but often have unanswered questions that are unrelated to the illness. The questions have more to do with the future in relation to themselves. Parents rarely talk with their children about specific plans for the family after the parent dies. Teenagers ask, "What's going to happen around the house? Will my Dad go with someone else or is he going to stay with us or what is going to happen to us?" Although they have questions about the future, they are also uncertain about whether they really wish to have answers to those questions: "I think I'd rather have them as questions rather than find out. Because if they get answered I may not like them."

GUIDELINES FOR CARE

Practitioners need to appreciate that teenagers struggle with many paradoxes as they attempt to reconcile the fact that, if their parent dies, they will be catapulted into independence. At the same time, they resent their parent's illness as an obstacle to getting on with their own lives.

- Provide opportunities for the teenager to express the many conflicting feelings about their situation, knowing that if they describe one feeling they are likely harboring other, conflicting feelings. For example, if they express that they never think about the fact their parent will die, expect that they are also dwelling on the fear of their parent's death.
- Assist the teenager to feel closer to their ill parent by facilitating a family discussion, suggesting that they write their parent a letter, or make an audiotape in which they express their feelings toward their parent.
- Assist parents to understand their teenager's feelings within the context of normal growth and development.

CONTENDING WITH CHANGE

All members of the family living with terminal illness must face changes in their relationships, roles, responsibilities, social life, and health.

For teenagers, changes in roles and relationships are often experienced as a shift in dependency between themselves and their ill parent. Like adult children, teenagers experience a role reversal in their relationships with their parents. The child begins to parent their parents: "I suddenly realized I could no longer depend on my Mum as a mother anymore. She has become more of a friend to me or I am more like a mother to her. That feels kind of strange."

In the majority of families, spouses assume most of the physical care of the ill person, however, teenagers often assist with that care: "When he gets sick I always stay by him and offer him a glass of water and rub his back if he is throwing up." When most of the physical care needs fall to teenagers, they find this overwhelming. They express the need to have someone else close at hand "in case the worst happens."

Teenagers experience changes in socialization because they often spend less time with friends. Teenagers often feel the need "to get away" so that they can stop thinking about things at home for a while. They feel the urge to get on with their lives and not put everything on hold: "I just have to get on with my own life. I can't let everything else fall because of this."

Although they try to get on with their lives, teenagers experience changes in relationships with their friends. They feel they have to grow up faster than their friends and they perceive this makes them stronger:

> I think I had to grow up quite quickly but I just tell myself, "Well, this will make you a stronger person." I just say to my gossiping friends, "How can you waste your time on that? There's so much more to life."

Teenagers often describe their own health suffering since their parents became ill. They complain of stress-related illnesses such as headaches, fatigue, exhaustion, stomach problems, colds, coughs, and flu: "I have chronic headaches which the specialist told me was stress and I would have to just learn to live with it."

Performance at school declines for many teenagers as they find it increasingly hard to sustain their concentration: "I just can't keep my train of thought. I feel I should be spending my time with Dad rather than studying. I guess I am just really exhausted, wiped, physically and mentally."

GUIDELINES FOR CARE

The practitioner needs to understand that teenagers living with a terminally ill parent are contending with many changes in all aspects of their lives.

- Assist parents to access care providers if the teenager is having to assume much of the physical and emotional care of their parent. Help parents to understand how overwhelming this situation can be for their teenage children and assist them to set limits on the care the teenagers are expected to provide.
- Encourage teenagers to continue socializing with friends in order to pursue normal growth and development.
- Assess the teenager's health status particularly in terms of stress related illnesses. Identify ways to lower stress levels such as relaxation techniques or physical exercise and help the teenager to design their own stress management program. Refer to a physician if health problems are severe.
- Encourage parents to speak with their teenager's schoolteacher to explain the situation at home and to adjust courses and assignments, as necessary.

SEARCHING FOR MEANING

Searching for meaning involves making sense of the situation and putting the experience into some context. Teenagers, like all family members, search for meaning in their situation and often ask the question, "Why me?" They wonder why serious illness has struck their family. Their questions often center around worrying about a future without their parent.

As a result of impending independence, many teenagers experience fear of the future. The independence teenagers are seeking is one over which they have control; the independence resulting from their parent's death is one they cannot control. Teenagers also experience a sense of urgency to get on and establish themselves in the world "while the going is good." There is a significant threat to teenagers' security as they try to comprehend the meaning of their parent's death in terms of its effect on their own futures.

As they search for meaning and acknowledge their own vulnerability, teenagers rarely resolve to take better care of themselves as adult children tend to do. Rather than engage in health-promoting behaviors, teenagers frequently engage in self-destructive behaviors.

Teenagers often believe that getting cancer is based purely on chance and that one's own health behaviors have little bearing on the development of illness: "Just happening to get cancer, or happening to get hit by lightning, or happening to win the Lotto 649. Those are so much due to luck." Although teenagers may believe that getting cancer is due to chance, they also feel their parent has a responsibility to get well. Teenagers are often extremely judgmental if, for example, their parent continues to smoke in spite of their poor state of health:

> I don't really hope that he'll get better because he still continues to smoke and he drinks alcohol with his pills so he's not taking care of himself, and if he really wanted to, or at least help, he would stop.

Teenagers do not usually demonstrate much reflective thinking about the illness in relation to their own values and attitudes. Teenagers' thinking tends to be more concrete and revolves around a basic survival need for security for themselves.

GUIDELINES FOR CARE

Practitioners need to appreciate that the teenagers' search for meaning centers on their fear of the future without their parent. Fear of the future triggers resentment in teenagers that their parent could do more to help the situation.

- Communicate your appreciation of their fears about the future. Help them to find ways to alleviate the fear, understanding what triggers it and what relieves it.
- Allow them to ventilate their frustration and resentment toward their parent for not behaving in ways that would promote health. Role play with them about ways to communicate their concern to their parent rather than their resentment.

LIVING DAY TO DAY AND PREPARING FOR DEATH

Some families eventually begin to live from day to day and prepare for death. Living day to day is characterized by making the most of the time left and accepting the way things are rather than worrying about the future.

Teenagers rarely focus on living day to day and preparing for death. Because of their developmental drive for independence and their need to get on with their lives, teenagers have difficulty focusing on the day at hand:

> I live for tomorrow. I always try and push this out of my head so it's not something I think about every day. You just have to keep your chin up and keep focused on your other things and realize that life's got to go on and what's going to happen is going to happen.

Accepting that death is close at hand triggers a great deal of fear about the future. By not thinking about their parent's eminent death and focusing on their own lives, they protect themselves from fear which helps them to get on with their own lives.

GUIDELINES FOR CARE

Although other family members may be preparing for death and living day to day, the sensitive practitioner can expect that teenagers may need to shield themselves from the knowledge of their parent's impending death. Consequently, practitioners can predict that the teenager may be extremely shocked and upset at the time of death.

- Acknowledge teenagers' need to shield themselves as a protection from the reality of a future without their parent. However, it is also important to give sensitive information as to how imminent death is.
- Expect that teenagers will not be fully prepared for death because of the way they have shielded themselves from this reality. If possible, therefore, a skilled individual should be available at the time of death and after to assist teenagers deal with their feelings.

SHIELDING: THE ESSENCE OF TEENAGERS' EXPERIENCE

The conceptualization of fading away provides a useful framework within which the experience of teenagers who are living with a terminally ill parent can be described.

The underlying theme for teenagers is their intense drive to put their own lives ahead of others and to get on with doing the work of adolescence. Although teenagers make an effort to be available for their ill parent by spending more time at home, and by assisting with some aspects of physical care, they view the situation as a hindrance to getting on with their own lives.

Encountering this hindrance brings on a host of emotional reactions for teenagers as they perceive themselves as being held back in their lives. Fear is a common emotion underlying many of the behaviors and actions of these teenagers. To ensure continuation on their developmental path and to protect themselves from fear, teenagers shield themselves from the reality of the inevitable death of their parent. They shield themselves by choosing not to think about the situation, and by maintaining their view of their parents as they were before they became ill. When the shield is lowered at times, for example, when their parent's physical symptoms worsen, teenagers often become overwhelmingly fearful because the security of their future is in jeopardy. Shielding protects teenagers from facing a reality for which they are not ready.

Caring for a family with teenagers can be very challenging for all practitioners. Appreciating that the experience of teenagers is similar in some ways and yet different from those of other family members, helps practitioners provide interventions that are specific and effective for family members at different developmental stages. Assisting family members to manage their personal situation will ultimately help the family as a whole cope with a difficult time as they prepare for the death of their loved one.

REFERENCES

1. R. E. Grinder, *Adolescence*, John Wiley & Sons, Inc., New York, 1973.
2. D. K. Wellisch, Adolescent Acting Out when a Parent has Cancer, *International Journal of Family Therapy, 1*:3, pp. 230-241, 1979.
3. H. Berman, C. E. Cragg and L. Kuenzig, Having a Parent Die of Cancer: Adolescents' Reactions, *Oncology Nursing Forum, 15*:2, pp. 159-163, 1988.
4. E. Rosenheim and Y. Ichilov, Short-term Preventive Therapy with Children of Fatally-ill Parents, *Journal of Primary Prevention, 3*:6, pp. 67-73, 1981.
5. J. A. Daniels, Adolescent Separation-individuation and Family Transitions, *Adolescence*, Vol. XXV:97, pp. 105-116, 1990.

CHAPTER 10

Family Functioning*

Palliative care practitioners operate on the principle of caring for the family as a unit during a terminal illness, but they often struggle with how to put it into practice. To be effective, the practitioner needs an accurate understanding of how the family normally functions as this profoundly influences how families experience the transition of fading away.

We found that families in the study experienced the transition with greater or lesser difficulty, depending on their level of family functioning. How families interact according to the following eight dimensions contributes to their success or difficulty: integrating the past, dealing with feelings, solving problems, utilizing resources, considering others, portraying family identity, fulfilling roles, and tolerating differences. These dimensions occur along a continuum of functionality so that family interactions tend to vary along the continuum rather than being positive or negative, good or bad.

DIMENSIONS OF FAMILY FUNCTIONING

Integrating the Past

Previous experience with illness, loss and other adversity influences family members in their current situation. For some, painful experiences in the past contribute to their growth and help prepare them for future adversity. They acknowledge the pain and trauma associated with the past event, but incorporate what they learn into subsequent experiences, including the current terminal illness.

For example, Mr. X. had been forced to hide from the Nazis during World War II. Despite the intensity of this experience, Mr. X.

---

*This Chapter is an adaptation of, Davies, B., Reimer J., and Martens, N. (1994). Family functioning and its implications for palliative care. *Journal of Palliative Care, 10*(1), 29-36. Reprinted with permission.

interpreted it not as a pervasive negative event but an experience from which he could learn:

> I have had that experience . . . I have found that even with hard times, you can go on. It's amazing what you can do even in hard times. You don't give up. You do what you can do, and that's about it.

Family members may describe traumatic events of the past, but they also recount enjoyable experiences from which they gained pleasure. They reminisce about shared family experiences and appreciate the positive interactions they had with the ill person and each other.

In contrast, in some families, members hang on to past traumatic experiences and continue to dwell on the painful feelings associated with the event. Mr. Y, for example, believed he had been persecuted by his church and retained a sense of bitterness and pain. He felt deserted in his present situation.

These family members often direct their energy to "recreating" the past so that they have happy memories. One daughter, for example, felt as though she had been abandoned by her mother. Now, as her mother was dying, this daughter described, with extreme intensity, her attempts at recreating the mother-daughter relationship she felt she never had: "I just lie beside her and cuddle her . . . I just can't let her go."

Dealing with Feelings

Some families express a range of feelings, from happiness and satisfaction, through uncertainty and dread, to sadness and sorrow. They describe their feelings, and express their vulnerabilities, and fears: "The happiness is not here that there was a short while ago. We both are very, very sad with what's happened."

When anger is expressed, it tends to be in relation to a specific event in the patient's care, and usually involves the failure of the medical community to respond appropriately. The anger is part of the story the family tells; they are not still angry and do not dwell on the negative aspects of care: "You wouldn't believe what happened there . . . anyway that is a long story, and I don't like to think about it any more. We're in another hospital now, and they are very nice."

Members acknowledge their vulnerabilities and their paradoxical feelings about the patient's continued decline. They describe their ambivalence about what is going to happen and their response:

"I'm trying to prepare, but maybe you can't prepare. But, how do you prepare for this anyway?"

In contrast, some families do not acknowledge their uncertainty nor talk about the paradoxes they face. They appear to avoid the feelings of turmoil associated with pending death. Instead, they shield themselves from the pain, often hinting that they do not express what they feel.

Such families often describe a narrow range of feelings, with more intensity associated with anger, hurt, and fear. Anger is the most common and pervasive feeling expressed. Mr. T., for example, used frequent profanity when describing the behavior of other people and expressed anger in response to even the most neutral questions.

Solving Problems

Some families identify problems as they occur and openly exchange information. Members agree upon possible solutions. They participate in problem solving, remain open to suggestions and implement alternative strategies creatively. Often members acknowledge and appreciate the contributions of each other, which results in a sense of support and togetherness.

They seem to take control of the situation, resolve the problem, and put the issue aside while they retain the lessons learned:

> At home we were following directions . . . phoning and not getting anywhere, and meanwhile Dad was getting tremendous pains. I was really very frightened for Dad. Finally we phoned the ambulance and just took Dad down to the hospital . . . if that ever happens again, we will just call the ambulance.

In contrast, other families appear to agree on issues in a group interview because they do not contradict one another. However, in subsequent individual interviews, family members elaborate on their view of the problem, and blame other family members for lack of, or inappropriate, actions. For example, in one family interview, members agreed that the doctor's failure to return their calls was the source of the problem of pain control for the patient. In the individual interviews however, the daughter blamed her stepfather for contributing to the problem because he gave too much of the wrong kind of medication.

These families approach problems by focusing more on why the problem occurred and who was at fault than on generating potential solutions. They seem so caught up in the emotions associated with the situation that they can not act on the problem. They often feel persecuted, or singled out to receive poor treatment. "You phone the doctor and ask for a return call . . . and I don't get a phone call back. How do you think I feel? I want to kill somebody."

They often seem unable to communicate what they expect from the health care system, and then when their expectations are unfulfilled, they are angry. They may also have a sense they cannot influence care or make changes. For example, one daughter recounted a problem with her mother's care. She indicated she could do nothing about the situation and imagined what the response would be if she even tried:

> I feel like really stirring up a lot of things—but what's the point? . . . You know that nothing's going to happen. The nurses are going to say, "Your mother just got a little upset . . . make sure you're a little nicer to your mother when you visit".

Utilizing Resources

Some families utilize a wide range of resources. They receive considerable family support and identify many friends or acquaintances who offer help, particularly emotional support and empathy. They seem open to accepting this support and express satisfaction with the results.

They seek suggestions concerning resources and take the initiative for locating other services as needed. One family phoned drug stores and health care workers repeatedly until they tracked down an anti-nausea bracelet.

Other families utilize few resources. Members appear reluctant to seek or accept help. The assistance they receive comes mostly from formal sources rather than informal support networks. They describe fewer friends and acquaintances who offer assistance. And, when they receive assistance, they appear dissatisfied.

Considering Others

In some families, members show concern for each other and acknowledge the extra responsibilities involved with caring for the ill member. They express concern and compassion for one another. For example, one brother perceived that his sister was carrying most of the load in caring for their mother: "My sister is probably doing a lot more . . . it's affected her household, I think, more so than mine because she does a lot of running around."

These families tend to focus their concern on the patient's well being. If the patient is well cared for, then other family members are satisfied. They do not express needs for personal attention from health care practitioners, though they appreciate individualized attention when it is given. This contrasts with families that tend not to recognize the extra responsibilities assumed by other family members. One patient expressed no awareness of the extra load his wife was assuming although she was exhausted. The focus of each individual tends to be his or her own emotional needs. Each person in the family appears alone in the experience, or misunderstood by the others. One daughter, when asked who supported her, replied,

> No one, just myself. I don't get along with my brother, I never have. He's mean to me in an emotional way. My father has let me down. I'm alone in a world where I know all these people.

Some family members explicitly state their desire for having somebody meet their needs, to care for them: "One nurse actually took an interest in me and sat down and talked to me one day and every time I came in she'd ask me how I was doing."

Because of the focus on individual needs, these families cannot fully respond to the patient. One daughter, for example, spoke repeatedly of how much it meant to her to be with her mother, without referring to the mother's needs:

> In the last four months she (the patient) never got mad at me, she never got grumpy. I talk to her on the phone or at home and if I come I just know how much I mean to her and how much she loves me and it's just so neat.

Portraying Family Identity

Some families are able to agree on the characteristics of their family; the family has an identity of its own that is acknowledged. For example, a family's philosophy might direct all members to do their best to manage each situation with courage and strength. Statements about the family and individual members are generally positive, and they express and demonstrate warmth and caring. Members frequently compliment one another on their sensitivity and contributions.

The family provides the individuals with a nurturing and supportive environment which carries with it feelings of safety and trust. When recounting events, family members demonstrate agreement among themselves and all family members participate in the discussion. They often clarify and openly correct each other until they think the situation has been described accurately. Views expressed in a group correspond with views held individually.

Family members who do not clearly identify family characteristics tend to talk more about their personal characteristics than how they see the family. There is often discrepancy between what is acknowledged as the truth in group interviews compared to what is expressed in the individual interview. One person may dominate the group interview, and provide his or her view of the event in an authoritative way with minimal contribution by the other members. There is little correcting or clarifying of one another. Then, in individual interviews, family members offer their own version of the event. Understandably, families try to maintain some guise of closeness, an image of a warm, caring family, when in fact, there may be considerable hostility and possibly a history of sexual, physical or emotional abuse. Outward appearances are not congruent with reports of what is actually happening, or has happened, within the family.

Prior to the illness, families in which members work well together report a pattern of visiting with one another on a regular basis in addition to celebrating holidays and special family occasions together. They describe a history of closeness in the family. The current situation reinforces these previous patterns; members visit even more often and frequently indicate they have grown closer.

Other families do not have regular contact and closeness prior to the palliative care situation. They are brought together by the current situation and provide little evidence that this regular contact will continue following the patient's death. Instead, they indicate that members will return to previous patterns of contact.

Fulfilling Roles

Some families allocate household and patient care responsibilities in a flexible way. For example, a daughter helps her parents with their laundry and meals, the son does outside work, and the grandchildren help with the lawn so that the spouse can devote time to caring for the patient. Spouses indicate they have readily taken on the care of their husband or wife, and see this as their primary responsibility. They express satisfaction with their decision to dedicate more time and effort to the patient.

In contrast this may not be possible for some families and members tend to maintain their previous roles and responsibilities. There is a sense that they do not adapt easily to the new situation and do not accept roles being taken over by others, particularly "outsiders" such as homemakers or community health nurses. For example, despite major physical changes, one patient struggled to maintain his pre-illness level of activity, with total disregard for his safety. The patient's care is not shared by family members. There is more resentment surrounding the patient's care, either in feeling obligated and unsupported in providing care, or in being critical of others: "My brother came into town for a few short days and ripped me apart because I wasn't there full time taking care of (mother)."

Tolerating Differences

In some families, a positive dynamic exists which permits and encourages members to express differing opinions and beliefs about various issues. For example, the daughter of one family indicated her religious faith was very strong, while the son acknowledged that his faith was less than the rest of the family, and that was acceptable. Such families are also more tolerant of others outside of the family. They understand their good intentions even though they do not agree with the approach or advice offered:

> All those people who tell nice stories of friends who died of cancer . . . that is the most horrible thing they can do, but they do it with good intentions, so what can you say? Just listen to them . . . still they are good friends.

In contrast, some families tend not to express differing viewpoints in a group interview. They express their discrepant views in individual interviews and tend not to tolerate differences. "Mom and Dad want me to talk, so they keep talking to me and I start snapping at them. I don't just come out and say that I don't feel like talking right now." The patient replied harshly, "Well, maybe that's what you should do if you don't feel like talking . . . You don't want to converse with me, but you want to know all the answers and don't mind asking questions. . . ."

Different approaches by friends or health care workers are not easily tolerated either.

> One friend phoned and told me how he felt, and he says he can't deal with it, there's just no way. He said he'd see me outside of the hospital and have a cup of coffee with me. Forget it, I don't have time. If you can't deal with it, I can't deal with you either.

Table 1 summarizes the eight dimensions of family functioning and gives examples of the range of behaviors evident in each dimension.

This table summarizes those behaviors that, on one end of the continuum are more helpful, and on the other end, less helpful to families facing the transition of fading away.

Table 1
Dimensions of Family Functioning:
Examples of the Range of Behaviors*

Integrating the Past

describe painful experiences as they relate to present experience	describe past experiences repeatedly
describe positive and negative feelings concerning the past	dwell on painful feelings associated with past experiences
incorporate learning from the past into subsequent experiences	do not integrate learning from the past to the current situation
reminisce about pleasurable experiences in the past	focus on trying to "fix" the past to create happy memories which are absent from their family life

Dealing with Feelings

express a range of feelings including vulnerability, fear and uncertainty	express predominately negative feelings, such as anger, hurt, bitterness, and fear
acknowledge paradoxical feelings	acknowledge little uncertainty or few paradoxical feelings

Solving Problems

identify problems as they occur	focus more on fault finding rather than on finding solutions
reach consensus about a problem and possible courses of action	dwell on the emotions associated with the problem
consider multiple options	unable to clearly communicate needs and expectations
open to suggestions	feel powerless about influencing the care they are receiving
approach problems as a team rather than as individuals	approach problems from individual perspective rather than as a family
	display exaggerated response to unexpected events
	withhold or inaccurately share information with other family members

*Originally published in, Davies, B., Reimer, J., and Martens, N. (1994). Family functioning and its implications for palliative care. *Journal of Palliative Care, 10*(1), pp. 35-36. Reprinted with permission.

Table 1 (Continued)

Utilizing Resources

utilize a wide range of resources	utilize few resources
open to accepting support	reluctant to seek help or accept offers of help
open to suggestions regarding resources	receive help mostly from formal sources rather than from informal support networks
take the initiative in procuring additional resources	
express satisfaction with results obtained	express dissatisfaction with help received
describe the involvement of many friends, acquaintances and support persons	describe fewer friends and acquaintances who offer help

Considering Others

acknowledge multidimensional effect of situation on other family members	focus concern on own emotional needs
express concern for wellbeing of other family members	fail to acknowledge or minimize extra tasks taken on by others
focus concern on patient's well being	
appreciate individualized attention from health care professionals, but do not express a strong need for such attention	display inordinate need for individualized attention
direct concerns about how other family members are managing rather than with themselves	
identify characteristic coping styles of family unit and of individual members	describe own characteristic coping styles rather than the characteristic way the family as a unit coped
demonstrate warmth and caring toward other family members	allow one member to dominate group interaction
consider present situation as potential opportunity for family's growth and development	lack comfort with expressing true feelings in the family group

Table 1 (Continued)	
Considering Others (Continued)	
value contributions of all family members	feign group consensus where none exists
describe a history of closeness among family members	describe few family interactions prior to illness
Fulfilling Roles	
demonstrate flexibility in adapting to role changes	demonstrate rigidity in adapting to role changes and responsibilities
share extra responsibilities willingly	demonstrate less sharing of responsibilities created by extra demands of patient care
adjust priorities to incorporate extra demands of patient care and express satisfaction with this decision	express resentment over perceived lack of support in caregiving
	refer to caregiving as a duty or obligation
	criticize or mistrust caregiving provided by others
Tolerating Differences	
allow differing opinions and beliefs within the family	display intolerance for differing opinions or approaches of care giving
tolerate different views from people outside the family	demonstrate critical views of friends who fail to respond as expected
willing to examine own belief and value systems	adhere rigidly to belief and value systems

Guidelines for Care

Palliative care is an applied discipline that depends upon a sound knowledge base and excellent clinical skills. Research is the means by which information is generated that can describe the complex concerns, issues, and problems that families face and can suggest

appropriate interventions based on fact. Despite the fact that literature on care of the dying is growing, approaches for care of the family
tend to be described in a general way. Practitioners often find that
traditional practices are insufficient to deal with the complex issues
and interactions of families caring for a terminally ill member. The
assessment guide and the intervention strategies which follow were
derived from information families provided about having a member
terminally ill with cancer and receiving care either at home or in
hospital. As such, the interventions are based on family members'
direct accounts of their experience, the problems they faced, and the
things that helped or hindered their ability to cope.

Assessing Family Functioning

A prerequisite for working with families in palliative care is an
assessment of family functioning. Such an assessment enables practitioners to be more effective in their interactions with families. The
eight dimensions of family functioning described in Table 1 provide
a guideline for this assessment, and for determining an appropriate
plan of care. For example, some families spend considerable time
reviewing painful aspects of their past during the current caregiving
situation and this can interfere with optimal care for the patient.
Similarly, because of their history, some families find they cannot
pull together as a unit to cope with the stress of palliative care. In
families where there is consensus about the problems, open and
direct communication, and flexibility toward change, the practitioner can approach the family as a cohesive unit. In other families
where communication is indirect, little agreement about the nature
of the problem exists, roles are rigidly entrenched, and there is little
tolerance for differences of opinion, practitioners cannot approach
the family as a cohesive unit. Instead they must consider other
approaches, such as directing attention to each family member
separately.

To a great extent, assessing family functioning depends upon
communication with the family. Practitioners must recognize that
members of some families may be reluctant to share differing viewpoints in the presence of one another. Practitioners need to obtain
information from more than one family member and gather data
over time as some families may reveal critical information only
when they have developed trust.

Part of understanding the family includes having family members tell their story. In some families, the stories tend to be repeated

and feelings associated with them resurface. Practitioners need to spend considerable time listening and acknowledging these feelings. Talking about the past may be a "way of being," a pattern to be understood, not necessarily a signal for therapeutic intervention. Practitioners need to use their clinical judgment to determine whether someone tells a story because he or she wants to be better understood, which is most often the case, or because he or she seeks help with the issue. This distinction is important. When the person is telling the story for the purposes of being better understood, then discretionary non-action is the most appropriate approach. When the person telling the story is seeking help with the situation, then practitioners provide therapeutic intervention or make the appropriate referral.

Finally, negative perceptions of past experience leave some families hypersensitive to interactions with the health care system. These families do not easily tolerate any change or unforeseen circumstance that interrupts plans. Consequently, issues related to the competence, reliability, patience and persistence of palliative care practitioners assume great importance. For example, failure to promptly return a phone call may result in an angry response which can erode the trust that is building.

Solving Problems

Palliative care practitioners as a "rule of thumb" often present families with a variety of options so they may choose what suits them best. This approach works well in cohesive family units. However, in some families, solving problems takes considerable effort on the part of the family and the practitioner. The family's level of functioning will influence how practitioners obtain and share information, offer resources, and determine particular approaches.

Obtaining and sharing information is crucial for problem solving. Practitioners may need to gather information from more than one family member as they may perceive the situation differently and may not feel comfortable sharing disparate views in a group meeting. Also, practitioners cannot assume that information shared with one family member will be openly and accurately shared with other family members. Practitioners may have to repeat answers to the same questions from various family members.

In offering resources, considerable attention needs to be given to the degree of disruption associated with the suggested change. For example, the introduction of a homemaker may seem a reasonable solution to accomplish extra tasks. From the family's perspective however, introducing someone who does things differently from the normal routine may be viewed as more of a strain than a help. Practitioners need to make an extra effort to ensure the best possible fit between the family and the resource. For example, a family that is dissatisfied with a particular homemaker might cancel the entire service and perceive the experience as yet another example of failure of the health care system to meet their needs.

Family conferences are commonly used to help families solve problems and this may work well with some families. However, depending upon their level of functioning, some families may not follow through with the decisions even though consensus seems to have been achieved. Though not voicing their disagreement, family members who do not see the problem in the same way, may not be committed to the solution put forward, and will disregard the plan.

Finally, practitioners often use support groups for assistance with emotional and practical issues. These groups are helpful for those who benefit from hearing the perspective of others in a group. However, these groups may not necessarily be appropriate for family members who require more individualized attention. Instead, they may require one-to-one interactions with a practitioner with whom they have established trust.

In summary, the family as a whole dies along with one of its members—it will never be the same again. Every aspect of the family's life and functioning is undergoing change, a change imposed against its will. Inevitably, these changes create stress within the family. The way a family has functioned in the past profoundly influences the way it deals with the dying of one of its members.

For some families, the stress of palliative care coupled with their decreased level of family functioning makes the situation almost overwhelming. The expectation that they will "pull together" to cope with the stress of palliative care may be unrealistic. It is essential that practitioners not judge such a family but appreciate that the family is coping as best it can under the most trying of circumstances. For this reason, the practitioner needs to work with the family as it is, rather than imposing expectations about what the family "should" be and how it "should" cope. These families need support and affirmation of their existing coping strategies, not judgmental criticisms. Moreover, alternative suggestions for coping can only be effective when the family perceives that their present coping strategies are compounding their stress rather than relieving it, and are ready to change their existing patterns of functioning. The challenge for practitioners is to use their knowledge, skills, support, affirmation, and patience to assist the family through the crisis in a manner that supports the integrity of the family as much as possible.

CHAPTER 11

Location of Care*

Patients with advanced cancer receive care in a variety of settings: home, hospice, hospital, or continuing care facilities. Parkes was one of the first researchers to document differences for patients and family members related to palliative care at home, in hospice units, and in hospital units [1-3]. More recent studies focus on family satisfaction with care or indicators of quality care in different settings [4,5].

When family members differ in their preferences for location of care, conflict results, but generally, families prefer palliative care at home unless they feel out of control. The success of home care relates to four factors: an able and available caregiver; comprehensive and reliable home care resources; the patients's physical condition; and a suitable home environment. Family members may feel out of control when they lack adequate knowledge and skill to care for the patient, when they feel fatigued, or when they have insufficient home care resources. Then, they prefer hospitalization as a way to regain control. This relieves the total responsibility of patient care. They perceive the hospital as a resource with skilled and knowledgeable staff who can assess and respond to any situation with technology that can help control the patient's symptoms.

BENEFITS OF HOME CARE

From the family's perspective, the home environment facilitates a sense of normalcy, sustains relationships, and contributes to reciprocity between the ill person and family. The home environment allows the ill person to just "be there" in the center of patient and family activity and the point of connection to friends and

*This Chapter is an adaptation of, Brown, P., Davies, B., and Martens, N. (1990). Families in supportive care—Part II. Palliative care at home: A viable care setting. *Journal of Palliative Care*, 6(3), 21-27.

community. The patient can continue with established patterns of interaction. As one person said, ". . . at least being at home she still has a finger on the pulse of the world."

Family members often define normalcy with their own unique set of criteria. For instance, one daughter defined this in terms of her mother's ability to play the piano. Another patient expressed normalcy as the ability to smoke and have coffee with his "cronies." The family lives as normally as possible despite the illness and its ramifications. The patient eats meals with the family, and family members continue with regular patterns of school and work. Normal routines continue free of the sights, sounds, and smells in a hospital setting.

Normalcy should not be confused with avoidance or denial. Patients and families recognize their situation but use distractions to put death-related thoughts aside. The home enables periods of normalcy, which facilitates coping.

The home environment also helps sustain relationships within the family and with friends. Family visits to the patient at home do not entail juggling time and responsibilities as do visits to the hospital. Friends can phone or visit more easily than in the hospital where it appears too many visitors come when the patient is ill and too few when the patient is ready for more company. The ease with which interaction takes place at home contrasts sharply with visiting in a hospital. "In the hospital, with her roommate there, you can't have an intimate conversation. At home, whenever you do need her to talk to, or somebody to talk to, she's there."

Patients and families equate care at home with freedom and control. They have some degree of self-determination. Patients can rise, bathe, dress, eat, and visit according to their own routine. The hospital cannot accommodate that luxury and families must conform to routines and regimens. Self-determination can play a role in symptom control. For instance, favorite foods at home may result in an improved nutritional status, or the patient may choose to lie on the floor to relieve chest and back pain. Patients prefer the home environment, ". . . because I've got my own things around me and I can do things I want to do when I want to do them and don't have to live to a timetable."

Family members identify reciprocity as another benefit from home care. Participation in home care engenders gratifying reciprocity between the ill person, family and friends and creates opportunities for "shared awareness."

THE SUCCESS OF HOME CARE

Four factors determine the success of home care: the availability and skill of the caregiver; comprehensive and reliable home care resources; the patient's physical condition; and a suitable home environment.

Able and Available Caregiver

Family members recognize the viability of home care rests on the presence of a willing and able caregiver. Patients are well aware of the physical, psychological and social burden family caregivers experience. Family members, while reluctant to describe the experience as burdensome, nevertheless suffer some social isolation, a sense of being tied down, role overload, and physical fatigue.

Comprehensive and Reliable Home Care Resources

The abilities of family members in the caregiving role align closely with the type of support received from local home care programs. Non-professional or support services such as homemaking, personal care, companion sitting, together with the appropriate medical equipment, alleviate the caregiver's workload. However, these services help only if provided to the extent the family believes necessary, otherwise great frustration results. As one caregiver said, ". . . unfortunately, her illness doesn't go away on the weekends, so I think if she's having hygienic care Monday to Friday, those needs would still be there on Saturday and Sunday." Caregivers also see twenty-four-hours-a-day, seven-days-a-week accessibility to and availability of physicians and visiting nurses as crucial for symptom control.

Patient's Physical Condition

Family members identify the patient's physical condition, especially in relation to mobility and symptom control, as critical to the success of home care. As long as the patient remains mobile and manages elimination, home care remains feasible for the patient and for family members. Families express concern about their ability to manage a bed-bound and/or incontinent patient.

Patients and other family members both agreed that care at home was more desirable when the patient was feeling well than when the patient's symptoms were not being adequately controlled.

For example, family members found twenty-four hour pain control regimens confusing and families were often attempting to operate highly technological equipment such as patient controlled analgesia pumps. The highly emotionally charged issue of nutritional support for the anorexic patient weighed heavily upon families.

Suitable Physical Environment of the Home

Finally, the physical environment of the home represents a crucial aspect of home care success. Stairs limit the patient's mobility within the home and access to the outdoors. Patients experience difficulties with a wheelchair in a small kitchen or a walker on carpet. Families cannot always meet the challenge of home adaptation.

HOSPITALIZATION

The decision to hospitalize the patient arouses a variety of emotions that range from guilt and anxiety to fear. Families see hospitalization as necessary when the situation gets out of control. Families define "out of control" as when the patient becomes too ill, the caregiver lacks the necessary skill, or becomes fatigued.

Some families view the patient as too ill to be cared for at home when she/he can no longer mobilize independently and needs assistance to turn in bed, to transfer from one place to another and to carry out basic activities of daily living. Immobilization, in turn, affects the patient's ability to manage elimination. Incontinence is another factor which may precipitate hospitalization.

Uncontrolled pain is another circumstance that families identify which may lead to hospitalization. Families cite this reason less often than loss of mobility and inability to manage elimination.

Families also feel out of control when the caregivers lack adequate knowledge and skill to care for the patient. They clearly express concern that their care may be inferior to hospital care. As one family member said,

> I can't make him as comfortable in bed as the nurses here do. I watch and see the way they look after him and the way they position him and I've tried to do the same thing. I don't achieve the same results.

Finally, caregiver "burn-out" is another reason families feel hospitalization may be required.

In summary, the patients and family members involved in this study preferred care at home over hospital care because the home environment facilitated being there, normalcy, self-direction, sustaining relationships, and reciprocity. Benefits of home care, however, can be realized only when there is a willing and able caregiver, when the patient is not "too ill," when the physical environment of the home can be adapted to meet the patient's needs, and when home care services are provided to the extent required.

REFERENCES

1. J. Cameron and C. M. Parkes, Terminal Care: Evaluation of Effects on Surviving Family of Care Before and After Bereavement, *Postgraduate Medical Journal, 59*, pp. 73-78, 1983.
2. C. M. Parkes, Home or Hospital? Terminal Care as seen by Surviving Spouses, *Journal of the Royal College of General Practitioners, 28*, pp. 19-30, 1978.
3. C. M. Parkes and J. Parkes, "Hospice" versus "Hospital" Care Reevaluation after 10 Years as seen by Surviving Spouses, *Postgraduate Medical Journal, 66*, pp. 120-124, 1984.
4. B. Beck-Fris and P. Strang, The Family in Hospital-Based Home Care with Special Reference to Terminally Ill Patients, *Journal of Palliative Care, 9*:1, pp. 5-13, 1993.
5. L. Kristjanson, Indicators of Quality of Palliative Care from a Family Perspective, *Journal of Palliative Care, 1*:2, pp. 8-17, 1986.

CHAPTER 12

Challenges of Conducting Research in Palliative Care

While conducting the research reported in this book, we encountered many challenges. Palliative care studies, by their very nature, pose significant challenges to the researcher. Cassileth points out that "the fragility of patients and their physical or cognitive limitations severely curtail the types of studies that are possible and the research methods that can be applied" [1, p. 5].

There has been virtually no discussion of the challenges of conducting qualitative research in palliative care. This is perhaps not unusual given that "symptom and psychosocial research have been assigned a low priority in most cancer centers" [1, p. 7]. Psychosocial research in palliative care has only recently received much attention, but discussion is most often directed toward quantitative approaches [1, 2].

In retrospect, we recognize that many of the issues which presented as challenges for this research are not unique. However, we share our experience in this chapter in order to heighten awareness of the issues so others undertaking similar research might anticipate them and determine creative ways of handling them.

SELECTING THE APPROPRIATE DESIGN

Determining the most appropriate and feasible research design was complicated by the severity of illness and the complexity of the patient and family situations. The research originated from the concerns of nurses who were providing palliative care to patients and their families in both home and hospital settings. The nurses' goal was to provide optimal care to patients and their families, but they identified a lack of knowledge upon which to base family-focused care. The ultimate goal of the research therefore was to optimize the care for dying patients and their families by more clearly understanding their experience.

RESEARCH METHOD

Qualitative Approach

One challenge facing psychosocial research in palliative care concerns how best to measure the variable of interest, and with what instruments. Ideally, following the selection of the factors to be studied, a standard measurement instrument with good validity and reliability would be applied [1]. Facing this challenge forced us to reconsider the overall research approach.

When first examining the problem for this study, the researchers identified factors which influenced the family's response to palliative care. We thought that a quantitative design would be most suitable, so that the variables being tested could be quantified and statistically analyzed. Based upon a thorough literature review and upon the clinical experience of the investigators, an extensive list of independent variables potentially relevant to the family's experience with palliative care were identified. Instruments with potential for measuring most variables were located. However, given the severity of illness and the sensitive nature of palliative care, asking families to complete a myriad of questionnaires was deemed inappropriate. Only one or two instruments could have been selected for families to complete, but the team was interested in exploring the families' experience as a "whole," rather than predetermining one component of the experience on which to focus. Moreover, some of the psychosocial scales were developed and normed on college students or psychiatric patients, groups that have little in common with the terminally ill. Some wording and questions would have to be changed. Also, the normative data from such standard scales were not useful as norms for palliative care patients. Finally, the available instruments were taken from a variety of disciplines; there existed no conceptual or theoretical framework which would draw them together in a meaningful way. Thus, it became evident that the uncritical reliance on preexisting research instruments would preclude a true exploration of the research question and would result in limited conceptualization, premature closure, and doubtful utility. The misapplication or untimely use of theories from many disciplines would produce only a superficial fit between theory and reality, approaching the problem for the top down (from theory to practice), rather than from the ground up (from practice to theory) [3].

A similar dilemma surfaced in our attempt to define the dependent variable. If, for example, a family stress-coping framework were used, "coping" would be the logical dependent variable. However, coping may not be the only, or the most important, aspect of the family's experience. Moreover, although the instrument of choice for measuring coping was logically derived from clinical experience and literature review, it was not grounded in the experience of families themselves.

It is generally agreed that the choice of method in research investigation should be determined by the research question. In addition, as Siegel stressed, it is vital to select a research design that is suitable for the state of existing knowledge about the questions being asked [4]. Therefore, we decided that the method of choice for the research program must be one which asked the families themselves about their experience with palliative care. Qualitative methods were deemed most appropriate; specifically, the procedures of grounded theory were employed.

The use of a qualitative research design versus quantitative approach resulted in difficulty gaining approval from one agency to conduct the research at their hospital. Citing the traditional arguments against the validity and reliability of qualitative research due to the small self-selected sample, the hospital in question would only consider approving the proposal if essentially the design was changed to that of a quantitative study.

Prospective Approach

Traditionally, the family is seen as the first external resource to which the cancer patient turns for support when facing advanced cancer. The entire family, however, may be in crisis when one of its members is receiving palliative care. It is appropriate, therefore, to view the family unit as the focus of palliative care. In fact, one of the basic tenets of palliative care is that the unit of care is not just the individual patient, but the family.

The relevance of considering the families' experience with palliative care is based upon the view that the family is an open system of interdependent individuals with patterns of mutual interaction and exchange. Factors affecting one individual also affect others in the system. As such, the admission of one family member to a palliative care program affects other family members. However, few studies systematically document the family's experience. Most studies have been done retrospectively using interviews with family members after the patient's death, and most frequently, with only one family member, usually the surviving spouse. The patient, however, is central to the family's experience; it was, therefore, deemed essential that the patient be included in the research. The contribution of patients may be limited by the disease itself, cerebral metastases, confusion, medication or other forms of treatment. Because of this, other family members are often used as informants, but there is always the risk of bias, conscious or unconscious, in the reports that they offer [2]. Cassileth warns: "Particularly in palliative care, using a family member to provide information about issues such as the patients' pain status or psychological well being is so confounded that it should be avoided" [1, p. 7]. Including the patient meant that the design was necessarily prospective. This had the added advantage of overcoming one major disadvantage of retrospective research: reliability tends to diminish with long term recall.

Cassileth's warning applies also to family level research: one cannot be certain that the information obtained from one family member is precisely consistent with what would have come from the other family members. However, it was deemed important to obtain data about the family from more than one individual member. Most families in palliative care programs are "older," that is, the average age of patients is sixty-five years. Therefore, for the study to have optimal relevance for these programs, families included the patient, spouse, and one child over eighteen-years-of-age. Interviews were held with the family group and with each member individually.

Requesting the participation of several family members places additional demands on families, making it challenging to find families willing to participate during a difficult time in their lives. Furthermore, asking families to participate in a group interview with other family members was stressful for some families. When families are already in situations that are stressful, this request may be overwhelming and may prevent some families from agreeing to participate. However, families who did participate in the group interview stated that they found it helpful to have the opportunity to talk together about the illness and about their reactions, even though the discussion stimulated painful emotions to resurface.

In any inductive research approach, an important step is to validate the ongoing analysis with the participants to ensure the interpretation accurately portrays their experience. Including the patients in a prospective design lead to another challenge: patients did not usually survive very long past the interview. Consequently, there was no opportunity to return to some patients to validate the data as they were either too ill or had died. Validation, therefore, had to be addressed in other ways, specifically by talking with other patients and families in similar situations.

RECRUITING SUBJECTS

Recruitment of subjects for the research presented one of the greatest challenges. Subject recruitment occurred over several months for each component of the project. Several external factors contributed to this lengthy duration including, for example, a nurses' strike which resulted in additional responsibilities for the nursing staff at the agencies involved in this project. More relevant to this discussion, however, were the difficulties encountered in identifying potential families.

All agencies who were involved with the research fully supported the project and were willing to assist with the recruitment of subjects. Participation in the research team by agency personnel facilitated this process. In the first phase of the research, however, agency support for the project was not adequate at the "grass roots" level. We held several individual and group meetings with staff who were working with potential subject families to provide them with detailed information about the study and the involvement required of participants. We offered information about the interviewers to reassure staff of the interviewer's communication skills and sensitivity. Even still, recruiting subjects by the staff was difficult. The staff reasoned that patients should not be approached because they were in a terminal stage, were too uncomfortable or in pain, were sleeping a lot, or had been "through enough." It seemed as though nurses were reluctant to tell patients or families about the study as they were protecting the families from a seemingly stressful imposition at a sensitive time. Eventually, we facilitated the identification and recruitment of families by directly involving a member of the research team in reviewing the patient kardexes and lists with a staff member.

As we progressed to subsequent phases of the research in other agencies in other cites, we realized that frequent and consistent communication was necessary with the staff about the project. Having an agency-based person as a member of the research team was instrumental in identifying appropriate subjects. In addition, face-to-face contacts with the staff, including physicians, were most helpful in explaining the purposes and procedures of the study. Ensuring that the staff knew the interviewer and had confidence in her skills was also critical to making the staff comfortable in approaching patients for the study.

Difficulties in obtaining patients were also related to the family members' needs. In some situations, the patient was willing to participate but the spouse wished to "protect" the patient and, therefore, refused. Some families refused because they had participated in other studies or had simply been "through too much." Even when families were recruited and had consented to participate in the study, we encountered other problems. Two families, for example, agreed to participate but the patients were too ill to participate at the time of the interview. Another family agreed to participate but the patient died before it was possible to conduct the interview.

There was also the challenge of ensuring that the staff were not just referring those families who needed particular help, perceiving the interview as an opportunity for such families to ventilate in some therapeutic way. It is important in qualitative research of this type that participants represent as wide a range of experiences as possible so that all types of families were included, not just those with problems.

The challenges with recruitment reinforced our concerns regarding the ethical conduct of research, specifically the "risk-benefit" equation. Although most social scientific research does not place subjects in situations which directly and overtly jeopardize their health and well-being, most psychosocial research does involve some risks. Emotional discomfort, anxiety, and revelation of intimate secrets are all possible costs to subjects of becoming involved in a research project. These risks are compounded in family research where there is the additional risk of exposing family secrets. No investigator should think that it is possible to design a risk-free study, nor is this expected of researchers [5]. Rather, the ethics of human subject research require that investigators calculate the risk-benefit equation, or balance the risks of a subject's involvement in the research against the possible benefits of the project (both to the subject and to the society).

As clinicians and researchers, our primary commitment was to the patients and their families at a critical point in their lives. Families are under much stress; they are facing one of the most difficult situations that any family encounters. They have little time left to spend together, and we were asking them to share some of that precious time with us. The ultimate goal of the research was to enhance the quality of life for other patients and their families, but were we jeopardizing the quality of life for those who participated in the study? On the other hand, was there a greater risk in *not* doing research and increasing the knowledge base upon which we provide care to families in palliative care?

We took steps to minimize the risk to participants, such as selecting only patients whose clinical status was such that they were capable of participating. In addition, we were reassured by the reports of others which stated that one principal reason for patients' interest in research is their desire to make a contribution through their illness experience to the well-being of others [6]. Moreover, we believed that their participation might even have the potential benefit of adding to the quality of their remaining life. Such beliefs, however, could not justify putting families at risk for additional discomfort if we found that the interviews were too difficult for them. Consequently, we carefully followed guidelines for the ethical conduct of research, which included fully explaining the study to participants, reassuring them that they were under no obligation to participate and that they could withdraw from the study at any time should they wish to do so. In addition, each interview concluded with the question, "What has it been like for you to take part in this interview?" Responses to this question indicated that all family members found the experience beneficial in several respects. For example, one patient responded, "It's almost like getting some of the things out into the open, . . . in a way it kind of helped us stop and think again of just where we're going." An adult child stated, "I don't mind answering your questions and I think I benefit from this, too, because I'm sort of being put into a position where I must put into words what I think and feel." Some participants indicated that the actual interview sessions were "difficult" in that they "were forced to face the facts." But, even these respondents perceived the value of the research indicating that the interview compensated for the temporary discomfort.

The responses reaffirmed that a search for meaning is common to individuals caught up by suffering. Participation in research provided an active role for the patient who may otherwise feel like a passive recipient of the care and attention of others. Family members also valued the opportunity to share their experience for the benefit of others. Vitally important to ensuring that families feel that their contribution is valued is how the families are approached and interviewed.

CONDUCTING INTERVIEWS

Interviewing patients and families in palliative care presents many challenges. First, we recognized that the participants in the study would be undergoing a period of considerable stress. Therefore, they were reassured when they were first approached about the study, when they signed the consent form, and at the beginning of and during each interview, that they could choose to stop the interview at any time. In addition, we recognized that it was critical that family members perceive the researcher as a knowledgeable and caring individual, someone who will respect the "ground rules": that participants will be protected as much as possible from any adverse consequences of their participation. Family members benefit when the interviewers exercise discretion and judgment in what is observed and probed, and when they conduct the interview sensitively and with discretion.

It is essential, therefore, that interviewers have the ability to conduct interviews in this way. After an initial period of hiring several interviewers, we were very fortunate in using only one interviewer whose work with the project was her primary professional interest for the duration of the study. This meant that her schedule was flexible enough to meet the requests of families for interview times and locations. In addition, it also had the advantage of providing consistency in approach and in data collection.

Interviewers must meet several requirements. We found it mandatory that interviewers have a solid knowledge base in family systems and group dynamics, and must be skilled in interviewing individuals and groups. They must also be knowledgeable about palliative care. Our interviewer was a masters prepared nurse with a clinical specialization in oncology/palliative care; she understood the illness, the treatments, and the symptoms that patients were experiencing. Her clinical ear and eye were always attuned to the patient's and family's needs, and this helped families feel satisfied with their decision to participate in the interview. In a sense, she was an "insider," someone who knew the in's and out's of cancer care. As a result, she was able to enter the family system more easily than someone who was totally new to the experience. Interviewers must be comfortable with discussions of death; having interviewing experience with other kinds of sensitive issues is not necessarily transferable to interviews in which death is discussed. In addition, interviewers must be able to maintain objectivity in following interview guides, while also being sensitive. They must be able to cope with the emotional drain of the interviews and the analysis process.

Interviewers require adequate orientation, followed by some form of ongoing monitoring through regular discussion to help prevent over involvement with families. Debriefing sessions are also required so that interviewers have opportunities to share their own reactions and express their own emotions stemming from such intimate contact with families during a critical time of life.

When a family member is seriously ill, the entire family is affected. Their schedule is altered, their responsibilities are increased, their time is limited. Meeting with the researcher then is one more task that must be added to the list. Interviewers, therefore, must be willing to meet with the family on their terms, at the time and place that is most convenient for them. Considerable time was required to set up interviews because the patient's condition changed quickly and the interviewer did not want to be an added burden or come at times inconvenient for the patient and family. The interviewer was as sensitive as possible to the needs and conditions of patients and families, and the length of the interviews was guided by the reactions and needs of patients and families.

Even when families agreed and wanted to participate in interviews, the interviewer faced challenges pertaining to continuing with, or prematurely stopping, the interview. One patient, for example, insisted on finishing the interviews because of her hope that the information would help others. The interviewer, however, sensed this patient was experiencing considerable pain and offered to stop the interview. The patient refused to stop, expressing her desire to continue. Upon completion of the interview, the patient indicated that the hardest part of the interview had been that it was "very draining." In another situation, when an interview needed to be interrupted so the patient could be repositioned more comfortably, the interviewer wondered how much longer the interview should be continued. She knew that if the interview was concluded prematurely, there would not likely be another opportunity to complete the interview. The patient seemed comfortable and so the interview continued, but weighing the data's value to the study against the participant's discomfort was an ongoing struggle for the interviewer.

It was challenging for the interviewer to separate clearly her roles of researcher and clinician. This can be a particular problem in family research where the therapeutic ambience of the interview may predispose participants to cast the interviewer into the role of therapist [5]. The interviewer had to guard against mentioning anything in an interview with one family member which was mentioned in the interview with another that had not been mentioned in the group interview. We learned that the group interview was best done after individual interviews because family members had had the chance to say what they wanted, in confidence, to the interviewer before meeting in the large group. That way, too, the interviewer was prepared for anything that might come up in the group interview that she knew would be difficult for an individual member. The interviewer had to guard against putting herself in the position of supporting a particular point of view in the family, no matter how much she personally subscribed to it. She worked very hard at remaining sympathetic but neutral since the intent of the interview was to talk with the family as a whole, and with individual members, to learn about their experience, however they perceived it. The intent was not to diagnose problems, or improve, or intervene in any way. Families who were assessed as potentially benefitting from therapy were referred back to the head nurse of the agency which identified the patient so that such families were offered a route for assistance should they desire it.

By conducting the interviews in the home, the researcher is selecting an informal atmosphere and thus wittingly or unwittingly encouraging friendliness, trust, and self disclosure. This predisposes the family to perceiving the interviewer not as a researcher, but as a clinician, or even as a friend. Many families went to special effort to offer tea, coffee, or cake as they would to a guest, not a researcher. Some families asked the interviewer to come back again for further discussion because they found the interaction meaningful. It was very important to make it clear to the families what the purpose and parameters of the interview were so that families did not expect that follow-up would occur. As a result, sending thank you letters for their participation was considered appropriate; sending sympathy cards after learning about the patient's death was considered inappropriate since such an act extended the relationship beyond the research. Adhering to this decision was sometimes difficult, especially in families were a close bond had formed during the interviews.

As indicated earlier, the interview may be emotionally charged for patients and for family members. Similarly, interviewers may also be affected by the emotion of the situation and perhaps

Appendix I

RESEARCH DESIGN

The purpose of this study was to examine the impact on families having a member with advanced cancer who was receiving palliative care either at home or in the hospital. This research is consistent with the fundamental principles underlying palliative care programs in which it is recognized that patients with advanced disease and their families require special care. The entire family is affected when one of its members is in need of supportive care. It is appropriate therefore to view the family as the unit facing the terminal care situation and as a focus of supportive care.

Benoliel was one of the first health care professionals to draw attention to the needs of the family of terminally ill patients [1-3]. Still, families' experience with palliative care has seldom been comprehensively investigated. For example, in a comprehensive review of the literature which examined the impact of cancer on the family, fifteen published studies conducted between 1975-1985 are discussed [4]. Not included were case analysis studies of patient responses and analytical papers that offered only interpretive comments in the absence of the actual data. Only six of the reviewed studies focused on the late stage of the disease. In four of these six studies, the respondents were the spouses of the identified patient. One study included the spouse and the patient; a second used the spouse and children of the patient, but excluded the patient. Of the fifteen studies reviewed, only one researcher used the patient, spouse and a child; the focus was on newly diagnosed patients.

More recently, several authors have strongly advocated a family perspective in cancer care [5-12]. A considerable number of studies have focused on the needs of family members of patients during earlier stages of cancer [13-19]. Studies of family members and of nurses involved in care of the terminally ill have increased our

understanding of families' experience [17, 20-22]. These authors con-
clude that, although family-focused care often implies that health
professionals must view the family as a unit, one cannot view the
unit as a whole without giving consideration to the individuals who
make up the unit.

Nurses and other health care professionals are finding themselves increasingly involved in providing palliative care. Despite the
fact that literature on care of the dying is growing, caring for the
family continues to be described in a general way. In order to design
appropriate interventions for family support, professionals who offer
palliative care must have an understanding of the impact upon the
family when one of its members is in need of palliative care due to
advanced cancer. Consequently, this study was designed to examine
prospectively the experience of families with advanced cancer in one
of their members.

METHOD

The choice of method in a research investigation is determined
by the research question. Qualitative methods are singularly
suited to research questions dealing with subjective experience and
perceptions with situational meaning and with areas where little
existing knowledge exists. Qualitative research involves the use of
an inductive approach, with no attempt to control for extraneous
variables or to place experimental controls on the phenomenon. The
particular qualitative approach used in this study was grounded
theory [23-26].

Grounded theory, deriving from the sociological tradition of sym-
bolic interaction, seeks to uncover the substantive social theory that
is embedded in everyday reality [23]. Consequently, grounded theory
was chosen as a means to build theory that would be faithful to the
experience of families with a member receiving palliative care. Thus,
theory would be grounded in reality and shaped by the situation in
which the families found themselves. It would reflect the complexity
of their experience and give evidence of the meanings families create
given the circumstance of palliative care.

SAMPLING

In grounded theory, the researcher is concerned with meaning or
content and not with distribution or frequency. Therefore, the most
appropriate sampling technique is a non-probability technique, that

of purposive or theoretical sampling. Using this approach, subjects are selected according to what the researcher needs to know.

A sample of twenty-three families (71 family members), who met the criteria, were selected from five sites: three home care programs, a supportive care program in a cancer center, and a palliative care unit in a general hospital. With a qualitative approach, the sample size is not as great a concern as it is with quantitative research [24]. Inter-relationships are sometimes better understood with a detailed study of a few cases and in fact, inter-relationships may be missed with the use of a large number of cases, especially when in-depth understanding is the goal. An additional rationale for small sample size is the fact that this approach requires great rapport between the researcher and the subjects, usually not achievable or desirable in quantitative studies. Furthermore, rapport is imperative in research dealing with sensitive topics like advanced cancer and impending death.

The patients were in the terminal component of advanced cancer and were receiving supportive or palliative care, that is, care given when cure and prolongation of life were no longer paramount and emphasis was on symptom control and quality of life. The terminal component usually lasts for a period of six months or less. Since very little is known about the trajectory of the terminal component, an attempt was made to obtain families who represented a range of times across this time period. Furthermore, families were accepted as subjects only if the patients had been in one of the palliative care programs for at least a week.

For the purposes of this research, "family" was defined as the family unit, including patient, spouse and at least one child. Most of the families who are in palliative care programs are older families; the average age of the patients is sixty-five. Therefore, families were not accepted into the research if the identified patient was a child. If the family had more than one adult child living at home, the child subject was selected at random. Families were considered potential subjects if they met the following criteria:

1. The family included a member who:
   a) had advanced cancer, that is, who no longer received curative therapies and who was identified by his/her physician as no longer an appropriate recipient of aggressive cancer therapy.
   b) was a patient in one of the palliative care programs and had been in the program for a minimum of one week.

      c) was judged by clinical personnel and the researchers as someone who would not be significantly burdened by participation in the study, that is, those with severe fatigue, uncontrolled pain or unresolved psychological issues were not approached.

      d) resided with his/her married or common-law spouse.

2. The family included an adult child (18 years or over) who lived at home or within a fifty-mile radius of the city.
3. The family members were able to communicate in English.
4. The family members were willing to participate in the study.

PROCEDURE

In obtaining the sample, the expertise of clinicians already familiar with the potential subject families was utilized. When a patient was identified who met the study criteria, the clinician approached the patient (and the spouse and adult child in person, where possible, or by telephone) and gave them a written description of the proposed study. If the potential subjects agreed, the investigator then contacted the family by telephone or in person to set up an appointment to meet with them, explain the study, answer their questions and obtain their consent to participate.

Interviews focused on how the family was managing the illness situation, the patient's care, and the family's perceptions of care at home and in the hospital. Interviews were tape recorded and the data transcribed verbatim. Field notes (both descriptive and reflective) were recorded by the data collector; theoretical memos were written which reflected the investigators' ongoing attempt to develop the conceptual aspects of the study. All data were subjected to content analysis, and constant comparative analysis, as described by Glaser and Straus [23] and by Straus and Corbin [26].

In the first and second phases of the study, family members were interviewed as a unit and individually. Because families represent more than a set of discrete individuals, a major issue in family research is the choice and use of the appropriate unit of analysis. Traditionally, family research has relied on one member of the family for information about family phenomena. In palliative care research, the informant is usually the spouse, most often the wife of the patient who died. To rely on only one perspective may result in a biased view of family phenomena. To include more than one member, however, results in other kinds of difficulties. For example, do researchers make conclusions based on data which reflects consensus or the majority of members with one perspective? Strategies for dealing with such problems have been discussed in relation to scored data [27], but little guidance exists for how to approach qualitative data. Consequently, our approach was to weigh each person's comments equally by analyzing all transcriptions, from both group and individual interviews, line by line, and often word by word. Our assumption was that all members' perceptions of the situation were equally relevant and contributed to the whole picture of the family.

ANALYSIS

Transcripts were read line by line, looking for codes, or words, that captured the meaning of the lines. In addition, each transcript was reviewed for commonalities and differences. Codes were compared with one another within the same transcript and with codes in other transcripts, and entire transcripts were compared with one another. "Selective coding" [25] guided the researchers to search for particular categories after developing provisional hypotheses that such categories represented important areas explaining the families' experiences. "Theoretical saturation" was reached when certain categories consistently emerged and no new information was discovered [26]. The codes were developed by the entire research team, and were refined as themes were discovered, illuminating family responses to palliative care. For example, one of the codes was labeled, "Integrating the past," and referred to those segments of the interviews in which individuals were describing elements of their past which affected the current caregiving situation. It was noted that this code appeared more frequently in some families. Ongoing analysis revealed other differences among the families. In examining these differences, it became clear that these differences were similar to descriptions used by other family researchers to describe patterns of family functioning [28-30]. Indeed, dimensions of family functioning captured the different ways which characterized families' experiences of the transition of fading away. These aspects are discussed in Chapter Nine.

The analysis of the first and second phases resulted in a theoretic scheme describing the experience of families with advanced cancer in one member. The families were in the transition from living with cancer to dying with cancer, the transition of fading away. The concept of transition is not a new one. Parkes proposed the concept of psychological transition which he defines as a change that necessitates the abandonment of one set of assumptions and the development of a fresh set to enable the individual to cope with a new altered life space [31]. The concept is also frequently used in human development literature [32], stress and coping literature [33] and nursing literature [1, 34]. In most discussions of transitions, it is acknowledged that they are initiated by stressful life events. Most often, these life events and their inherent changes are described as the beginning of transitions. In contrast, Bridges advocates that transitions start with endings, followed by a period of confusion and distress, leading to new beginnings in cases that have come that far [35, p. 9]. The experience of the study families followed this pattern of transition.

The third phase tested the conceptualization of the transition with five additional families who reported that the description of the phenomena made sense to them. This phase focused on assessing the rigor of the findings, using criteria applicable to qualitative research [36, 37], that is, criteria which make the interpretation "trustworthy." Credibility and fittingness were achieved through constant checking to ensure that the coding categories clearly portrayed the data as a whole, that the analysis contained both the typical and atypical elements of the data. Members of the research team kept each other honest by confronting one another and assisting each other to maintain distance from the data even while immersed in it. Independent coding of random interviews by two of the researchers also served to validate the findings. Finally, feedback solicited from colleagues in palliative care has indicated that the findings are reflective of their clinical experience with families.

PARTICIPANTS

A total of twenty-three families participated in this research program. Eight families were in Phase 1, ten in Phase 2, and five in Phase 3. In all families, the patient and spouse participated; and in all but two families, one child participated. In two other families, two children participated. In total, seventy-one family members were in the study.

The age range for both patients and spouses was from forty-six to eighty-five years. The length of time that the couples had been married ranged from three to forty-four years. Two couples were in their second marriage. The average length of time that couples had been married was 31.9 years.

In eleven families, the patient was the female member of the couple; twelve patients were male. Their diagnoses included cancer of the prostate, lymphatics, stomach, breast, lung, pancreas, ovary, bone and colon. Other sample characteristics are summarized in Table 1.

The time since diagnosis ranged from four years to eight months prior to the interview. Since the interviews were conducted, all patients have died.

Table 1. Characteristics of the Sample [N = 23 families]

Age Ranges	Patients	46 to 85 years
	Spouses	47 to 81 years
	Children	19 to 45 years
Duration of Marriage	Mean	31.9 years
	Range	3 - 44 years
Household Annual Income	< $20,000	3
	$20,000 - 39, 999	11
	$40,000 - 59,999	6
	> $60,000	2
	Not reported	1
Patient Gender	Male	12
	Female	11
Time Since Diagnosis	Mean	20.7 months
	Range	8 - 48 months
Source of Referral	Local Health Department - Home Care Program	13
	Supportive Care Program in Regional Cancer Institute	4
	Palliative Care Unit in Acute Care Hospital	6

Source: Davies, B., Reimer, J., and Martens, N. (1994). Family functioning and its implications for palliative care. *Journal of Palliative Care, 10*(1), page 29. Reprinted with permission.

REFERENCES

1. J. Q. Benoliel, Nursing Care for the Terminal Patient: A Psychosocial Approach, in *Psychosocial Aspects of Terminal Care*, B. Schonberg et al. (eds.), Columbia University Press, New York, pp. 145-161, 1972.
2. J. Q. Benoliel, Dying is a Family Affair, in *Home Care: Living with Dying*, E. R. Pritchard, J. Vollard, J. Starr, J. Lockwood, and A. Kutscher (eds.), Columbia University Press, New York, pp. 17-34, 1979.
3. J. Q. Benoliel, Health Care Providers and Dying Patients: Critical Issues in Terminal Care, *Omega, 18*:4, pp. 341-363, 1987-88.
4. F. M. Lewis, The Impact of Cancer on the Family: A Critical Analysis of the Research Literature, *Patient Education and Counselling, 8*, pp. 279-289, 1986.
5. D. Caruso-Herman, Concerns for the Dying Patient and Family, *Seminars in Oncology Nursing, 5*:, pp. 120-123, 1989.
6. P. F. Jassak, Families: An Essential Element in the Care of the Patient with Cancer, *Oncology Nursing Forum, 19*:6, pp. 871-876, 1992.
7. F. M. Lewis, Family Level Services for the Cancer Patient: Critical Distinctions, Fallacies, and Assessment, *Cancer Nursing, 6*, pp. 193-200, 1983.
8. J. Lillard and L. Marietta, Palliative Care Nursing, in *Toward a Science of Family Nursing*, C. L. Gilless, B. L. Highly, B. M. Roberts, and I. Martinson (eds.), Addison-Wesley, Redding Massachusetts, pp. 437-460, 1989.
9. E. J. Rosen, *Families Facing Death*, D. C. Heath & Co., Toronto, Ontario, 1990.
10. S. Schacter, Quality of Life for Families in the Management of Home Care Patients with Advanced Cancer, *Journal of Palliative Care, 8*:3, pp. 61-66, 1992.
11. K. B. Tiblier, The Family and Cancer, in *Toward a Science of Family Nursing*, C. L. Gilliss, B. L. Highly, B. M. Roberts, and I. Martinson (eds.), Addison-Wesley, Redding, Massachusetts, pp. 332-343, 1989.
12. S. Thorne, The Family Cancer Experience, *Cancer Nursing, 8*:5, pp. 285-291, 1985.
13. M. E. Grobe, D. L. Ahman, and D. M. Istrup, Needs Assessment for Advanced Cancer Patients and their Families, *Oncology Nursing Forum, 9*:4, pp. 26-30, 1982.
14. J. W. Hileman, N. R. Lackey and R. S. Hassanein, Identifying the Needs of Home Caregivers of Patients with Cancer, *Oncology Nursing Forum, 19*:5, pp. 771-777, 1992.
15. S. Jensen and B. A. Given, Fatigue Affecting Family Caregivers of Cancer Patients, *Cancer Nursing, 14,*:4, pp. 181-187, 1991.
16. K. Siegel, V. H. Raveis, P. Houts, and V. Mor, Caregiver Burden and Unmet Patient Needs, *Cancer, 68*, pp. 1131-1140, 1991.

17. K. Stetz, Caregiving Demands During Advanced Cancer, *Cancer Nursing, 10*, pp. 260-268, 1987.
18. C. A. Tringali, The Needs of Family Members of Cancer Patients, *Oncology Nursing Forum, 13*:4, pp. 65-70, 1986.
19. K. Wright and S. Dyck, Expressed Concerns of Adult Cancer Patient's Family Members, *Cancer Nursing, 6*, pp. 371-374, 1984.
20. L. Kristjanson, Indicators of Quality of Palliative Care from a Family Perspective, *Journal of Palliative Care, 1*:2, pp. 8-17, 1986.
21. N. Matens and B. Davies, The Work of Patients and Spouses in Managing Advanced Cancer, *Hospice Journal, 6*, pp. 55-73, 1990.
22. P. Skorupka and N. Bohnet, Primary Caregivers' Perceptions of Nursing Behaviors that Best Meet their Needs in a Home Care Hospice Setting, *Cancer Nursing, 5*:5, pp. 371-374, 1982.
23. B. G. Glaser and A. L. Strauss, *The Discovery of Grounded Theory: Strategies for Qualitative Research*, Aldine Publishing Co., Chicago, Illinois, 1967.
24. B. G. Glaser, *Theoretical Sensitivity*, University of California, San Francisco, 1978.
25. A. Strauss, Qualitative Analysis for Social Scientists, Cambridge University Press, Cambridge, England, 1987.
26. A. Strauss and J. Corbin, *Basics of Qualitative Research*, Sage Publications, Newberry Park, 1990.
27. C. R. Uphold and O. L. Strickland, Issues Related to the Unit of Analysis in Family Nursing Research, *Western Journal of Nursing Research, 11*:4, pp. 405-417, 1989.
28. J. J. Crosby and N. Jose, Death: Family Adjustment to Loss, in *Stress and the Family, Vol. II: Coping with Normative Transitions*, H. McCubbin and C. Figley (eds.), Brunner/Mazel, New York, pp. 76-89, 1983.
29. H. I. McCubbin and M. A. McCubbin, Typologies of Resilient Families: Emerging Roles of Social Class and Ethnicity, *Family Relations, 37*, pp. 247-254, July 1988.
30. D. H. Olson, D. H. Sprenkle and G. S. Russell, Circumflex Model of Marital and Family Systems, *Family Process, 18*:1, pp. 3-28, 1976.
31. C. M. Parkes, Psycho-social Transitions: A Field for Study, *Social Science and Medicine, 5*, pp. 101-115, 1971.
32. D. J. Levinson, C. N. Darrow, E. B. Klein, M. N. Levinson, and B. McKee, *The Seasons of a Man's Life*, Alfred A. Knopf, Inc., New York, 1978.
33. R. S. Weiss, Transition States and Other Stressful Situations: Their Nature and Programs for their Management, in *Support Systems and Mutual Help: Multidisciplinary Explorations*, G. Caplan and M. Killelea (eds.), Grune & Stratton, New York, 1976.
34. R. I. Mercer, E. G. Nichols and G. C. Doyle, Transitions over the Life Cycle: A Comparison of Mothers and Non-mothers, *Nursing Research, 37*:3, pp. 144-151, 1988.

35. W. Bridges, Transitions: Making Sense of Life's Changes, Addison-Wesley, Redding, Massachusetts, 1980.
36. E. G. Guba and Y. S. Lincoln, *Effective Evaluation*, Jossey-Bass, San Francisco, 1981.
37. M. Sandelowski, The Problem of Rigor in Qualitative Research, *Advances in Nursing Science, 8*:3, pp. 27-37, 1986.

Appendix II

The following are the guidelines used to conduct the interviews. In the first phase, we interviewed the family as a group prior to interviews with each individual member. In subsequent phases, we interviewed the individual members prior to the group interview. This change was made because it enabled family members to say what they wanted in confidence before meeting in the large group. The interviewer was also prepared for anything that might come up in the group interview that she anticipated might be difficult for an individual.

A. Phases I and II: Family Interviews

We believe that when a person is sick, like Mr./Mrs. X. (name), that there is an effect on the whole family. The greatest effect is probably on the person who is ill, but because we are all part of families, the rest of the family is also affected. We are interested in learning more about how families manage these kinds of situations, as a way of planning better care. Some people we are seeing are at home and some are in hospital, and we will be also asking questions about what it is like to be either at home or in hospital.

I. *I would like to begin by asking you some questions that have to do with how your family is managing this situation.*

1. For the past while, Mr./Mrs. X. has been very ill at home (in the hospital). What is it like for all of you to have him/her at home (in the hospital)? What kinds of things stick out in your mind about the experience?

119

2. When someone in the family is ill, there are often many things that must change. What have you had to change, to do differently as a result of Mr./Mrs. X.'s illness?

Probes (to be asked only if probes are necessary to stimulate the discussion):

a. What has changed in your jobs, tasks?
b. How have your feelings changed about the family?
c. When someone in a family is ill, we expect that their health requires much attention. Sometimes, the health of other family members is also affected. How has the health of the other family members been?

  i. Sometimes there is a recurrence of pre-existing health problems. Has this been the case for anyone in your family?
  ii. Sometimes family members have problems with every day concerns such as sleeping or eating or getting exercise. Have any family members had problems in these areas?
  iii. Sometimes family members find that they have difficulties carrying on their own social commitments and obligations. Has this been the case for any one in your family?

4. What, if any, other stressful events have happened in your family during this time? How have you managed? How are you managing these?
5. How does this situation compare with other stressful situations that you have experienced in your family in the past? How did you handle those situations?

II. *I would like to switch the focus now to questions about Mr./Mrs. X.'s care.*

6. What has been the most difficult part of caring for Mr./ Mrs. X. at home/ in the hospital?

Probes (to be asked only to stimulate discussion as necessary):

a. How have you managed these aspects?
b. What has helped or hindered?
c. Who has been involved in the situation?

     i. Who helps care for Mr./Mrs. X.?

     ii. Who comes to visit? Do they visit more at home or in the hospital?

     iii. What do they do that is helpful? Unhelpful?

     iv. In addition to friends and other people in the community, there have been other people involved in Mr./Mrs. X.'s care, such as doctors, nurses, and other health care workers. Who or what has been helpful to you? Unhelpful? How could they be more helpful or how could the services be improved?

     v. How have the services involved in the care been helpful? How could the services be more helpful, or how could they be improved?

     vi. Sometimes difficult times also bring out some good things for families. Have you experienced this? What are some of the good things?

III. *The next questions have to do with the location of care: at home or in the hospital.*

  7. When you think about Mr./Mrs. X. being at home or in the hospital, what do you see as the advantages and disadvantages of each?

  8. Can you see Mr./Mrs. X. going back to the hospital (going back home)? If so, what would make you want to do that, or consider that? If not, why not?

  9. Based on your experience, what suggestions would you have for other families who are going through a similar experience?

IV. *The last question has to do with your participation in this study.*

  10. Some families find that participating in a study like this is difficult; others like having an opportunity to talk. How has it been for you to participate in this interview?

Phases I and II: Individual Family Members (Spouses and Children)

Some of the questions I have for you are similar to the ones we talked about when I met with the group of you, and some are a bit different. When I met with your family, the questions were about the family as a whole. These questions focus on how you are managing this situation and how you see your family managing. Some of your responses may be the same as they were in the family interview, and some of them may be different.

I. *I would like to begin by asking you some questions that have to do with how you are managing.*

1. What has it been like for YOU to have Mr./Mrs. X. so sick this past while? What kinds of things stick out in YOUR mind about the experience?

   a. For adult child: What has it been like for your own family? Your husband/wife? Your own children?

2. When someone in the family is ill, many changes take place in the family. What have you had to change, or do differently, as a result of Mr./Mrs. X.'s illness?

II. *I would like to focus now on Mr. / Mrs. X.'s care.*

3. What has been the most difficult part for you in caring for Mr./Mrs. X.?

III. *The next questions have to do with location of care (at home or in the hospital).*

4. When you think about Mr./Mrs.X. being at home or in the hospital, what do you see as the advantages and disadvantages of each?

5. Can you see Mr./Mrs. X. going back to the hospital (going back home)? If so, what would make you want to do that, or consider that? If not, why not?

6. Based on your experience with your husband/wife/mother/father, what suggestions would you have for other families who are going through a similar experience?

IV. *The last question has to do with your participation in this study.*

7. Some people find that participating in a study like this is difficult; others find it interesting. How has it been for you?

B. Phases I and II: Individual Family Members (Patient)

Some of the questions I have for you are similar to the ones we talked about when I met with the group of you, and some are a bit different. When I met with your family, the questions were about the family as a whole. These questions focus on how you are managing this situation and how you see your family managing. Some of your responses may be the same as they were in the family interview, and some of them may be different.

I. *I would like to begin by asking you some questions that have to do with how you are managing.*

    1. What has it been like for YOU during the last while? What kinds of things stick out in YOUR mind about the experience?

    2. When someone in the family is ill, many changes take place in the family. What have you had to change, or do differently, as a result of your illness?

II. *I would like to focus now on your care.*

    3. What has been the most difficult part of your care?

III. *The next questions have to do with location of care (at home or in the hospital).*

    4. What has been the most difficult part for you (at home and in the hospital)?

    Probes (to be asked only to initiate discussion if necessary):

    a. How are you managing these aspects?
    b. What has helped or hindered you?
    c. Who has been involved in helping you?

        i. What do they do that is helpful, unhelpful?
        ii. What else might help?
        iii. How have the services involved in the care been? How could they be more helpful or improved?

    iv. As we said in the group interview, sometimes there are good things that come from an experience such as yours. Have you experienced any good things as a result of this experience?

III. *The next questions have to do with the location of care, at home or in the hospital.*

  5. When you think of being at home or in the hospital, what do you see as the advantages and disadvantages of each?
  6. Can you see yourself going back to the hospital (going back home)? If so, what would make you want to do that, or consider that? If not, why not?
  7. Based on your experience, what suggestions would you have for others who are going through a similar experience?

IV. *The last question has to do with your participation in this study.*

  8. Some people find that participating in a study like this is difficult; others find it interesting. How has it been for you?

C. Phase III: Interviews Guidelines (Families and Individuals)

As I discussed over the phone, I have several questions I would like to talk with you about. These questions arose from previous studies with other patients and families who were in a similar situation as you are. In our previous studies we noted that patients and families seemed to be going through a series of changes and reactions. We called this a transition and felt there were several components to this process of having a family member who was seriously ill. Within each of these components there were a number of things that the patients and families had to deal with, for example dealing with change, managing confusion and uncertainty, feeling like a burden, and so on. What I would like to do in our interview is to ask you some questions about how you view the transition and how your experience fits with this description.

  1. **Redefining:** When someone in a family has become ill and they're not able to function in their usual way, people begin to view them in a different way. In some ways, they're still the same, and in other ways, they are different. How has this been for you? What

things can you identify from your own experience that fit with this idea?

2. **Burdening:** When someone is ill, that person isn't able to do what they used to do so other members take on their work plus the responsibility of caring for the ill person. When this happens in families, people feel differently. Some people feel overworked and some don't; sometimes people protect each other or feel they're holding people up or holding them back. How has this been for you?

3. **Contending with change:** When someone in the family is ill, people can't always do their usual jobs, things are done differently, or people see things differently. Household tasks are handled differently, usual routines change. How has this been for you? How has your outlook changed? What other changes have you had to deal with? How has your health been?

4. **Struggling with paradox:** Some of the families found that when someone is seriously ill they feel like they are being pulled in two directions at the same time, for example, wanting to fight and wanting to give up, wanting to know answers and yet not wanting to ask the questions. What has been your experience? Would you agree that this occurs? How else might you describe this reaction?

5. **Searching for meaning:** In situations when someone in the family is very ill, people often try to find some meaning in the experience; they try to learn from what is happening to them. Has this been the case for you? What has helped you to deal with the situation?

6. **Living day to day, preparing for death:** Some of the families reported that there came a point when they realized that the patient was not going to get better; they then tried to make the best of things, to make the most of time. Others spent more time with the patient, and put things in order, for example, possessions, will, household information and so on. What has been your experience?

7. **Neutral zone:** People have told us that when someone is very ill, everything seems to be up in the air, on hold. They feel that they are in limbo, at a standstill, confused. Has this been true for you? How would you describe your experience, your reactions?

8. **New beginnings:** Some people have told us that there came a point when they realized that given the situation there were certain things that they wished to accomplish and that they could not let the situation overwhelm them. Does this fit for your experience? How would you describe your experience?

9. **Ending:** When someone is ill for a long time, people are always hopeful that the ill person will recover. Sometimes, there comes a point when people realize that ill person will not recover. Would you agree with this? Was there a point like that for you? What was it like for you?

10. **Transition of fading away:** We were trying to find a word or phrase which would help describe this process of dealing with a family member who is not going to recover. In our previous discussions with family members and patients, their descriptions of the patient seemed to suggest the person was losing ability and that this made them realize that the person was not going to recover. One person used the words, "fading away." We used the same phrase to describe this transition (show diagram). How does this fit your experience? How else would you describe it? What other words would you use? What is it that is fading away?

11. **Past experience:** Most of the people we talked to discussed their past experiences with illness, death or other major stresses in their lives and indicated that these all had an impact on how they handled the current situation. Is this true for you? In what ways have your past experiences impacted upon how you are handling this situation?

12. **Style:** In dealing with the whole situation, did you find that you recognized certain patterns of behavior that you and your family have used in the past to deal with other stressful situations? In dealing with the situation, have you used similar patterns or have you had to find new ways of dealing with this situation?

13. What else would you like to add to this interview? Is there anything else about your experience that would help us better understand this situation?

14. Would you think that this information might be helpful to other families? In what ways?

15. What might be the advantages and disadvantages of sharing this information with other families, or with health care workers?

16. What has it been like for you to participate in these interviews?

Appendix III

CASE STUDIES

The following case studies are examples of how two families faced the transition of fading away. The studies illustrate the transition as experienced by the patient, spouse, and adult child. They also illustrate how the members of these two families interact according to the dimensions of family functioning.

CASE STUDY 1

Eleanor and Jacob are in their late fifties. They have been married for just over thirty years. Eleanor combined a career as a librarian with raising four children: three sons and a daughter. The two eldest sons are working and living away from home. The youngest son and daughter, Melanie, live at home and attend the local university. Jacob has had a successful career as an engineer. Eleanor and Jacob have led an active social life and are fairly involved with their church and community. They had been talking more about retirement when Eleanor was diagnosed with cancer of the pancreas with multiple metastases to bone and liver.

In retrospect, Eleanor and her family identified changes in her health and stamina which they realized were indicative of her declining health. However, the realization still came as a shock when Eleanor's doctor confirmed that the pain she had in her right arm was another metastatic fracture. Although this was not the first she and Jacob had heard of the cancer spreading, they now realized that she was not going to get better. "You can't have cancer in your back, ribs, shoulder and now your arm and continue to believe you're going to recover. You know what you've got, you've got cancer, you're going to die from it."

Eleanor's Story

It's been terrible really, the ups and downs. You slowly start adjusting to it and you know, accepting it, and then, in my case, something else happens, it spreads to another bone. And it seems like, you know, as soon as I get on my feet I'm knocked down again. I don't know how long I can keep taking this. It's going to get to the point where it's going to be impossible.

If a person could have a second chance. It's even the way I view everything. Like my kids, I was always so hard on them because they don't pick up or don't do that. And yet, you know, now I realize how proud I am of them, because all four of them so far have turned out to be what I had hoped they would. What used to be important seems trivial. I used to be very interested in shopping and finding things for the house. The day after that clinic visit, I picked up my Canadian Living magazine and put it down because they were talking about how to rearrange your cupboards and I felt why look at that, it's not important anymore. Over the next few weeks what really reinforced for me just how ill I was getting were the drastic changes in my physical appearance. I've shrunk a lot, not a little bit. I have thought of myself as starting to disappear. You know my nose is getting closer to my toes because of the disintegration of vertebrae and bones and stuff. The pain is a constant reminder of what is happening to me. As soon as I start feeling a little better I almost get to the point where I forget what I have. When I feel worse, you know, that's when I realize what I really have. So I just take each day at a time and think every day is a day and sometimes I can do more and sometimes less. We're here for a short time and we're going to make the best of it.

As I lie here unable to care for myself and needing help to get to the bathroom, I worry that I am a burden to my family. They tell me I am not and not to worry, but I see my husband coming home from a full day at work and having to start supper. He may still be doing laundry at 10 at night. He's the one that gets me in the tub, he's the one that gets me my medication. Even going out is so much rigamarole. We went out Saturday night. He has to load me into the wheelchair and then they have to carry the wheelchair up four steps. So, I'm sitting there distracted by wondering how they're going to get me down the steps to get home. I don't want my kids to give up their activities with their friends to look after me, either.

Not only do I worry about all the extra work I am creating for them, I feel that because of me their lives are on hold. Our oldest son has a job offer out of town. I know that he is hesitating to accept because of me.

You want to give up and just curl up and wait, but because of the family you have to fight. I'm just trying to make sure I stay around, and when I feel so down in the dumps and tired I sometimes wonder what's the point of staying around? All of a sudden your life is not finished but you can't really think ahead. I've struggled with how much treatment to accept. I have thought of giving up the pills and the supplements and maybe not eating as much, but then every once in a while I think maybe a miracle will happen. When I start feeling like this, this is when some very special friends help me out. I can talk to them and cry with them. It's not that I don't share this with Jacob, but it's one less time he has to hear all this.

So I lie here and try to make sense of all this. As I said before, it has me thinking of things I never really spent a lot of time thinking about before. One thing it has done for us is to bring us closer as a family. We were always close but this has made us closer. We spend more time together, talking, laughing and just being in the same room. Now the kids seem to come and sit and tell me about all the things happening to them. They want to share it with you, and this bothers me, because, well, once I'm gone, who are they going to share it with?

Now that I know the future, I am making an effort to do some special things. I am trying to do some meaningful things with my family. I went to the Fathers' Day service at church. I didn't feel like it, but I thought, well it's Father's Day, who knows, this could be the last Father's Day that I will be in church. I am making some afghans because I thought it might be nice to leave something like that. I know this sounds morbid, but I bought a new dress the other day and told my husband he could use it to bury me. Now he won't have to run around looking for something.

Jacob's Story

Like Eleanor said, it was a shock. Perhaps not as much of a shock for me because I have been watching her and could see it was not getting any better. But it was still a blow. It was devastating to know that our time together was going to be limited.

Definitely, as Eleanor has described, she has under gone many changes in her physical appearance, mobility, and body functions. This has affected our physical relationship. I have had to adjust to all of this. But for me what is really important is keeping a relationship continuing. I put more emphasis on being together and talking than on going my own way and doing my own thing.

Sure, as Eleanor is now basically confined to bed I have had to take on a lot of the jobs she would have normally taken care of around the house, such as laundry, shopping, and cleaning. I used to work with a community league. I've given that up and use that time to do house chores. The kids are good about keeping their rooms tidy and starting supper. It's not a big deal, it's just the way it has to be. She gives me back as much as I give to her. We try to do things with as little fuss as possible to keep things as normal as possible.

The biggest help has actually been our friends. They have been bringing a lot of food and preparing meals, and making sure Eleanor has help to go to her appointments. These friends have also made visits and phoned her. They make sure the visits are spread out so she hasn't had much time to be depressed and it keeps her thinking. Certainly our life has changed because of the illness.

Normally I'd have gone out to the lake by now to open the cabin and hook up the water and all that, but we can't do that now. We used to go out for dinner on Friday night. We can't do that any more. I spend most of my time with Eleanor. If I have any struggle at all, it's with balancing my desire to be with her with my need to have some time to myself once in awhile. But, I'm lucky she understands that and encourages me to get out.

If I had my wish this would not have happened to us. But I have to admit there has been some positive to this situation. We were very close but it has drawn us closer. There are a lot of things the cancer has helped. Maybe we would have gone our own way and not paid attention to those things if Eleanor hadn't developed cancer.

Trying to make sense of all this has forced me to examine my faith and church beliefs. It's really reinforced to me my belief in the after-life. I couldn't cope with this if I did not have the belief that we will meet again. And I guess I sort of complain to God about this. I don't really benefit by talking to people other than Eleanor. I just sort of mull it over silently myself.

Like Eleanor said, and I agree, we really don't know if this will be for a long time or a short time, so you sort of take it day by day and spend as much time together as you can, and hope for the best. At work, there are a lot of different things to think about. So, it's not constantly on my mind. You have to put aside thinking about it, otherwise it would just depress you more.

When Eleanor told me she had bought a dress that we could bury her in, I brought up the issue of sorting out all the will and legal work. It was hard, but we went through that. I am glad we did because now things will be done the way Eleanor would like them. I've also made sure that Eleanor's friends know what to expect and, if I thought she wouldn't make it till Friday, I'd tell them to come and say good-bye. She may not be here the next time they come to visit.

Melanie's Story

It was exactly as Mom and Dad have described it. I felt like them, knocked down.

I think I'm having the hardest time adjusting to the changes in Mom's appearance. It's so hard to see her sleeping in her bed and just kind of withering away. I have always thought of her, as not invulnerable, but as a very strong individual. The hardest has been when you have to help her move. It sounds really dumb, but she was always really active and bounding around. It's really hard seeing her have so many problems moving. But, just because she doesn't look the same or do all the things she used to, I still need her to talk to. It's great to sit on her bed and tell her about my day.

You know it's funny, but this experience has really made me think about what I'm doing with myself. It's had some really good ramifications. It makes you realize that what you thought was important before, like whether or not you passed or failed in university, does not mean life is going to stop. Your future is important but you know that it is still going to work out in the end. Whereas, if she passes away, a part of you is missing after that.

Mom and Dad said we are closer as a family. My attitude toward my family has really changed. I used to want to be with my friends all the time. I wanted to have all this money so I could travel and buy things. But now you realize that your family is more important than any of that.

Dad's mentioned how much more work he has to do around the house, and I'm really trying to help him as much as I am able. At first it was hectic because she is a real perfectionist. It kept you on your toes and she wished we had ten hands so that we could get things done. It's hard for her to ask us to do so much. She was always the head of the family, but now she feels like she is being catered to. I was going to move out and live with my friends, but I have decided to stay at home. At first it was okay, but then after you have put everything else on hold for awhile, it gets pretty hard. Then you wish you were out somewhere, and then you feel guilty. You feel that you are being selfish because what's so important about going out at night when this is happening at home.

I think the pressure is starting to get to me sometimes, like it's easier for me to catch things going around. I find that I'm a lot more tired than I ever was before. You know, sometimes I'll be walking down the stairs and I'll get dizzy and weak.

I know about the plans Mom and Dad have made for her funeral, but it really didn't hit me that she wasn't going to be here until we went to a family wedding and Mom couldn't come. Like everybody else was there with their families, just everybody but her was there, and that felt really weird. I realized then that she wasn't going to be at family things in the future. So I'm trying to build myself up emotionally a bit, to be able to handle that when it does happen. You don't want to see the end, but you're getting ready. Sometimes you just turn to God and it helps you to feel there is going to be something happy for her after. There is going to be heaven and peace and the whole thing.

CASE STUDY 2

Ray and Donna are in their late sixties and have been married for forty years. Donna stayed home to raise their son, Ed. He is now thirty-five, a bachelor, living on his own, and employed as a mechanic. Ray is retired from a career as a finishing carpenter. Ray and Donna do not have many friends, and mainly keep to themselves. Ray was diagnosed with cancer of the esophagus with extensive abdominal metastases six months ago.

Ray's Story

It has been a bit of a shock. But not too much, because I have been like a yo-yo, going up and down, up and down. Like, suddenly I'm better, but I said let's not get hepped up on it, as I might go down again. And sure enough, I'm down again.

I've got it, I've got it. So? No big deal. As of now that's the way I see it. Because if you're getting weaker, you know that within three months from now you will be even weaker. I know I'm fading. When you are so damn weak, knowing the kind of power and strength you had before, why, I feel as if I'm a vegetable already. The Ensure might pick me up a bit, but it's just a matter of prolonging it. At first I didn't see it, but now I can see it. I'm all for putting up the good fight. You know what I mean? But, if you can't eat, you can't swallow anything, how are you going to fight? I don't believe in giving up, but I don't know.

But, all in all, nothing has really changed too much. Like, this past weekend, a neighbor helped me finish roofing the garage. It's all I could do to finish it. It just about killed me.

Because of all my problems, every step I take is a struggle. There are times I break down, but very, very seldom. I've faced reality, you know. But, I'm not going to complain about any of those woes or sicknesses to other people. I have no intention of talking like that. I'm just going to go through it.

I can still do some things. I can go upstairs by myself, and I can get my own cup of coffee. But, my wife is here and capable, and it's so much easier for her to do. I've always felt that the one that's sick is the one that's doing the suffering, so we should use our time to help them. Sure, I think there is some extra work for my wife, but I don't think it's all, all, all that much. My wife is very cooperative. She does what she can for me. She's a little crabby at times, but nothing to speak of cause whatever I want, she goes and does. My son helps her out by running errands like carrying groceries home. It's good that Ed is able to help out, not necessarily me so much, but he strengthens his mother.

Before you didn't think about death. Oh, momentarily you would, but not for long, because you were both well. Well, now we have had to talk about it. I've brought it up now and again, but not too often. We've made our arrangements. I guess each one of us are going to take it different maybe. I expressed my attitude toward dying and I can't live anymore. I've had a good life. I know that I'm not going to be living much longer and if we know that's there, why not accept it? I've given up thinking of the future because there is not too much to worry about in the future. I'm not going to be in any shape to do much about it. Why cry over spilled milk?

Donna's Story

I knew when the doctor looked down and said that they had removed fourteen malignant nodes, that it was the end. I knew then. It was devastating. Because not only is it their life, it's your whole situation and it means a whole new way of life for you. It's devastating because it's done away with everything you had planned for.

I have to rely on myself more now as Ray isn't able to do the things he used to. But he doesn't see this. He insisted on fixing the garage roof last weekend. I said, don't bother, it's good enough for another couple of years. But no, he wouldn't listen. He conned a friend into helping him. So now I won't even mention things that need to be done around here because if I do, he is going to want to do them. He's trying to do things that 15 years ago, when we moved into the house, he should have done. Now he's trying to do them when he can't. Now that I've realized this, I just leave everything until after. Because I know that it upsets him, disturbs him, that he can't be part of it, so why change it? But it's holding me up. There's times he gets up here and says, "I wish I would die. You want me dead. I know you want me dead. You're waiting for me to die." But I can't even talk to him about his sickness because he yells, "What do you want to know for? What's it matter to you?"

So I just say, well, I will continue to do what I can do and that's all I can do. But you're tied. He wants this, he wants that and he keeps calling me for it. Well, it's overwork because I'm not sleeping at night listening for him. It's hard. It's hard and it's not going to get any better. It's not going to get any better because he gets worse all the time.

I end up feeling guilty, because in a way I'm wishing everything was over and that I could get on with my life. But it's really not that way, you just get those feelings.

The good thing is that Ray's temper with our son is not so bad. He is calmer, he seems a little better with Ed; he'll talk to him a little bit more than he did before. Before he would just yell at him.

We've made our final arrangements. The final things I'll finalize myself later. But we talked about it and all you can say is that we hope we'll see each other later if it happens.

Cancer is this prolonged torture, mental and physical. It's a torture to everyone around you. If someone was to take another person and torture them, you would scream, you would yell, you would do everything. But here, we've got cancer doing that everything too, in families.

Ed's Story

It hasn't really hit me, as it's progressed through the months. I thought it would really upset me. I thought it would really break me down. I have broke down a bit, but I haven't to the amount that I thought I would. Basically, I haven't been crying, and I thought that I'd really cry.

It upsets me at times when I see him fall asleep sitting up. He's not as quick in the mind as he used to be. It's hard just seeing your

Dad deteriorating. But it's good that he can be home. He's here with his coffee, and he is in front of his TV, he's sitting on his couch. But it's hard for me to be here. It's hard to be home because it's pretty hard and that, and just real quiet.

Our life hasn't been the greatest, you know. We always had problems. But I think our emotional feelings for each other have changed. I feel we're getting along a little better. There's still the hard times and that, but we don't argue as much. Me and my Dad, we're a lot alike so we argue a lot, and we haven't been doing that as much. I don't think Dad's had the strength to argue as much, and he usually started the argument so we don't do that as often.

I guess the big change has been that my family really didn't need me as much before. They need me more now. So I really can't get on with my life, and figure out what I want. I guess as far as female companionship goes I think maybe I should go out, but I can't handle the time, and I don't want the hassle right now. If I could just get this behind me rather than just waiting, waiting, waiting.

Some days, I don't even want to show up to work anymore. I've just lost all interest. It feels like you don't want to do a thing. Life is at a standstill. I have no interests. I have no fun anymore. I feel I'm just waiting for something to happen to my father. I'm trying to progress with work, and I'm pushing myself to have fun. It's just I don't like putting stress on them. So I don't usually show my real feelings in front of my friends. I hide my true feelings.

Author Biographies

BETTY DAVIES has worked as a nurse, specializing in the area of death, dying, and bereavement for over twenty years. Her doctoral dissertation from the School of Nursing, University of Washington in 1983 and a postdoctoral fellow at the University of California—San Francisco in 1986 formed the basis for her seminal work pertaining to bereavement in siblings following the death of a child. She is a Founding member of the Board of HUGS Children's Hospice Society, whose major work is the establishment of Canuck Place, the first free-standing hospice for children in North America. In addition, she has conducted several studies in palliative care focusing on the families of both adult and child patients. The goal of her research is to translate research findings into practical terms as a means of achieving her goal of optimizing the care provided to those who are terminally ill and bereaved.

In recognition of her contributions to the field, Dr. Davies received the YWCA Woman of Distinction Award in Management and the Professions in 1991, and in 1993, received the Award for Excellence in Nursing Research and the Award of Merit from the Registered Nurses Association of British Columbia.

JOANNE CHEKRYN REIMER completed a Master's in Nursing degree from the University of Washington. Her studies focused on working with families where a member had advanced cancer and wished to remain at home during their final days. She worked in palliative care in several different capacities: as an Assistant Professor at the University of British Columbia, as the Hospice Nursing Consultant and Hospice Program Coordinator for the Vancouver Health Department Hospice Program, and currently as the Bereavement Care Coordinator for Canuck Place, a hospice for children in Vancouver, British Columbia. She has numerous publications that focus on family issues and cancer.

PAMELA BROWN graduated with a Bachelor of Science in Nursing from the University of Manitoba in 1980. Subsequent work experiences focused on care of the chronically and terminally ill with organizations such as the Victorian Order of Nurses Home Palliative Care Program. She completed a Master of Science in Nursing with a clinical specialization in palliative care at the University of British Columbia in 1986. She commenced work as a Clinical Nurse Specialist in Palliative Care at the Vancouver Health Sciences Center, and it was at this time that she began her involvement with the "Families in Supportive Care Project". In 1988, she moved to Calgary to assume her current position of Assistant Director of Calgary Health Services—Home Care Division.

NOLA MARTENS completed her Masters of Science in Nursing in 1988 from the University of Alberta. She has worked with families and patients with cancer for many years as a staff nurse and as an enterostomal therapist. She has also been involved with oncology nursing education and new staff training in a regional cancer institute. More recently, she was the Research Associate for the "Families in Supportive Care Project." At the present time, she is a research assistant for a study related to adolescent risk taking behavior.

Other Titles in the
DEATH, VALUE AND MEANING SERIES
John D. Morgan, Series Editor

Awareness of Mortality, *Jeffrey Kauffman*

Beyond the Innocence of Childhood: 3-Volumes, *David W. Adams and Ellie J. Deveau*

Vol. 1: Factors Influencing Children and Adolescents' Perceptions and Attitudes Toward Death, *David W. Adams and Ellie J. Deveau*

Vol. 2: Helping Children and Adolescents Cope with Life-Threatening Illness and Dying, *David W. Adams and and Ellie J. Deveau*

Vol. 3: Helping Children and Adolescents Cope with Death and Bereavement, *David W. Adams and Ellie J. Deveau*

Death's Critical Issues: Reflections in Studying Death, *Vanderlyn Pine*

Death and Spirituality, *Kenneth J. Doka with John D. Morgan*

Ethical Issues in the Care of the Aged, the Dying and the Bereaved, *John D. Morgan*

Fading Away: The Experience of Transition in Families with Terminal Illness, *Betty Davies, Joanne Chekryn Reimer, Pamela Brown, and Nola Martens*

Greeting the Angels: An Imaginal View of the Mourning Process, *Greg Mogenson*

Last Rites: The Work of the Modern Funeral Director, *Glennys Howarth*

Loss and Grief Recovery: Help Caring for Children with Disabilities, Chronic and Terminal Illness, *Joyce M. Ashton and Dennis D. Ashton*

Personal Care in an Impersonal World: A Multidimensional Look at Bereavement, *John D. Morgan*

Perspectives On College Student Suicide, *Ralph L. V. Rickgarn*

Spiritual, Ethical, and Pastoral Aspects of Death and Bereavement, *Gerry R. Cox and Ronald J. Fundis*

What Will We Do? Preparing a School Community to Cope with Crises, *Robert G. Stevenson*

Widower: When Men are Left Alone, *Phyllis Silverman and Scott Campbell*